A CASE TO ANSWER

A Case to Answer

*A first report on the potential impeachment of the
Prime Minister for High Crimes and
Misdemeanours in relation to the invasion of Iraq.*

Produced for
Adam Price MP

SPOKESMAN BOOKS

Authors of the Report
Chapter I: Glen Rangwala and Dan Plesch
Chapter II: Dan Plesch

With the assistance of Ffion Evans, John Fellows and Gwenllian Griffiths.

Glen Rangwala is a lecturer in politics at The University of Cambridge. He is the author if *Iraq in Fragments: the Occupation and Its Legacy*, to be published early in 2005.
Dan Plesch is an Honorary Fellow of Birkbeck College, University of London and a Visiting Senior Research Fellow at the University of Keele. He is the author of the recently published *The Beauty Queen's Guide to World Peace*.

www.impeachBlair.org

First published in August 2004 by Adam Price MP
House of Commons
London
SW1A 0AA

This edition published in October 2004 by Spokesman
Russell House, Bulwell Lane
Nottingham
NG6 0BT
England
Phone 0115 970 8318 Fax 0115 942 0433
e-mail elfeuro@compuserve.com
www.spokesmanbooks.com

ISBN 0 85124 704 0

A CIP Catalogue is available from the British Library

Printed by the Russell Press Ltd (phone 0115 978 4505)

Contents

A Case to Answer: A First Report

Foreword by Adam Price MP

* * *

Opinion

Foreword

This report sets out compelling evidence of deliberate repeated distortion, seriously misleading statements and culpable negligence on the part of the Prime Minister. This misconduct is in itself more than sufficient to require his resignation. Further to this, the Prime Minister's conduct has also destroyed the United Kingdom's reputation for honesty around the world; it has produced a war with no end in sight; it has damaged and discredited the intelligence services which are essential to the security of the state; it has undermined the constitution by weakening cabinet government to breaking point and it has made a mockery of the authority of Parliament as representatives of the people. The core conclusion of this report is that the impeachment of the Prime Minister has a strong basis in fact, and established precedent in parliamentary law.

It is on this basis that a number of parliamentary colleagues have declared their intention to bring a Commons motion of impeachment as an indictment of the methods, practices and conduct of the Prime Minister in relation to the war in Iraq.

This is a historic undertaking made with great regret but also a growing sense of resolution.

We are guided in this action by that most ancient of parliamentary doctrines: the principle of ministerial accountability, that those who lead us cannot mislead us and then remain in office. It is simply unprecedented for a minister to refuse to resign in the face of such compelling evidence.

All the usual constitutional conventions have been exhausted. Further inquiries into the Prime Minister's conduct have been refused. A vote of no confidence would bring all ministers within its scope and, therefore, fail to reflect the extent to which this Prime Minister made Iraq a matter of individual, not collective, responsibility, through the practice, as revealed by Lord Butler, not of government-by-cabinet but government-by-cabal. It is difficult to see why other ministers should find themselves in the dock when they were consistently kept in the dark through the actions of the Prime Minister. Finally, the normal rules of debate in the House of Commons mean that Members cannot accuse the Prime Minister of making misleading statements without immediately being required to withdraw the accusation. It is only by impeachment that Parliament will be able to discuss freely, and possessed of all the facts, the very serious issues raised by this report.

It is to history that Parliament has often looked when confronted by an unyielding executive. In 1628 the House of Commons sat in the ancient chapel of St. Stephens' following the King's rejection of the Petition of Right. Despite a catalogue of governmental disasters at the hands of the Duke of Buckingham, Speaker Finch was under an instruction "to interrupt any that should go about to lay an aspersion on the ministers of state." The Hansard of the day spoke of "a deep silence in the House." Sir Nathaniel Rich was the first to break it: "We must speak now or forever hold our peace. Shall we now sit still and do nothing and be scattered. Let us go to the Lords and show our dangers".

Sir Edward Coke, the reviver of impeachment, then rose to speak, telling of precedents in history when Parliament had spoken out against injuries to the State and to the liberties of the subject. A Parliament of Edward III had dared to name John of Gaunt - the King's own son - and members had gone to the Tower as a result. Under Henry IV, his Parliament had complained of the Privy Council. His words have a resonance that cascades down the centuries to the crisis of legitimacy we now face today:

> "Now, when there is such a downfall of the state, shall we hold our tongues? How shall we answer our duties to God and men? Why may we not name those that are the cause of all our evils? In the fourth year of Henry III and the twenty-seventh of Edward III and in the thirteenth of Richard II, the Parliament moderated the King's prerogative. Nothing grows to abuse but this House

hath power to treat of it…And therefore, not knowing if I shall ever speak in this House again, I shall now speak freely. I think the Duke of Buckingham is the cause of all our miseries. And till the King be informed thereof, we shall never go out with honour or sit with honour here. That man is the grievance of grievances. Let us set down the causes of all our disasters and they will all reflect on him."

For Coke and his allies, the impeachment of Buckingham was "the Cause of Causes", part of the long struggle by Parliament against executive abuse of power and to defend the fundamental principles of constitutional government. The Prime Minister, in choosing to prosecute a war on a false prospectus is guilty, like Buckingham, of "an act of transparent presumption and dangerous consequences". The choice that Parliament faces is whether it sits dumb-struck and dejected in the face of such monstrous abuse? Or will it rally to its ancient cry: let right be done as is desired?

To dust off Victorian constitutional histories and examine precedents from the time of Charles I and Chaucer may seem bizarre. But the conduct of the Prime Minister has left people and Parliament with no alternative if we are to preserve the very basis of our democracy. We are used to evasion, to spin and to economies with the truth. But to allow to go unchecked misleading conduct by the most senior minister, on so many occasions; about a war that will influence world affairs for decades to come; is to abandon the cause of liberty that has been so painfully fought for, established and preserved down the generations.

If his actions go unchallenged then we will have established a new constitutional precedent that will say that a minister can mislead the people and still govern with his conduct unpunished. Without the ability to enforce an honest account to Parliament on behalf of the people, there is no democracy. In this way our freedom dies.

When we hold this Prime Minister to account; when Parliament again becomes something more than a tourist attraction, then the United Kingdom government can again speak to the world with an honest voice and we can make some redemption for the disastrous policy that so many were deceived into supporting.

It is in that spirit that I commend this Report to colleagues.

Adam Price MP
August 23rd 2004

Introduction

1. This report was commissioned because of the great concern of Members of Parliament and the public over the misconduct of the Prime Minister concerning the invasion of Iraq and the apparent impossibility of any effective parliamentary accountability. The report details the Prime Minister's misconduct and finds that, all other constitutional remedies having failed, it would be possible for the Prime Minister to be impeached.

2. The first chapter of the report examines the statements and actions of the Prime Minister from September 2001 to August 2004 relating to Iraq. In particular, it finds that the Prime Minister:

– exaggerated the condition of Iraq's illicit weapons well beyond the assessments of the intelligence services or the United Nations inspectors. He asserted in early 2002 that Iraq had 'stockpiles of major amounts of chemical and biological weapons', whilst the assessment of the Joint Intelligence Committee at the time was that Iraq 'may have hidden small quantities of agents and weapons' (section 1.1);

– claimed that 'Saddam Hussein poses a severe threat not just to the region, but to the wider world' and had 'enough chemical and biological weapons remaining to devastate the entire Gulf region', whilst the intelligence assessment was that 'Saddam has not succeeded in seriously threatening his neighbours' (section 1.2);

– asserted that the 'UN proved' he had chemical and biological weapons because they were unaccounted for, in contrast to the warning by the executive chairman of UNMOVIC Hans Blix that 'One must not jump to the conclusion that they [weapons that were unaccounted for] exist' (section 1.3);

– claimed that Iraq's 'WMD programme is active, detailed and growing', even though he later admitted to the Butler review team that intelligence showed that 'what had changed was not the pace of Iraq's prohibited weapons programmes, which had not been dramatically stepped up' (section 1.4).

insisted that the invasion of Iraq was lawful because Iraq had committed a 'material breach' of Security Council Resolution 1441 by not cooperating with inspectors, even though Hans Blix told the Security Council that 'the numerous initiatives, which are now taken by the Iraqi side with a view to resolving some long-standing open disarmament issues, can be seen as "active", or even "proactive"' (section 1.5).

– claimed after the invasion that 'our intelligence' had confirmed that Iraq's 'two mobile biological weapons facilities' were part of a larger set of such facilities, even though intelligence had yet to examine the trailers, and then found them unconnected to biological weapons programmes (section 1.6);

– held back crucial information from intelligence sources that indicated that Iraq had destroyed its weapons stockpile (section 2.1);

– failed to ensure that intelligence sources were adequately checked, even when straightforward measures could have been taken to check those sources (section 2.2);

– claimed that the intelligence available to him was 'extensive, detailed and authoritative', even though he had been briefed by the Chief of MI6 about how key sources should be treated with caution (section 2.3);

– did not reveal the intelligence assessment in his possession that Iraq would be unlikely to use chemical or biological weapons outside its territory unless attacked first, despite the significance of this assessment (section 2.4);

– declared that the Iraqi declaration of December 2002 was 'false', even though he had not asked for that declaration to be analysed fully by the intelligence services (section 2.5);

– warned that 'it is a matter of time unless we act and take a stand before terrorism and weapons of mass destruction come together', even though the intelligence assessment was that the 'greatest terrorist threat to Western interests ... would be heightened by military action against Iraq', and the government was later forced to admit that 'the JIC assessed that any collapse of the Iraqi regime would increase the risk of chemical and biological warfare technology or agents finding their way in to the hands of terrorists, and that the Prime Minister was aware of this' (section 2.6);

– claimed in March 2003 that the contents of the September dossier 'still accurately reflect our assessment of the position with regard to Iraq's proscribed weapons programmes', even though those inspectors found a large number of the claims in it to be false (section 3.1);

– affirmed in January 2004 that 'the intelligence we received [prior to the war] is correct', even though the intelligence services had raised doubts about at least four key sources from at least six months earlier (section 3.2); and

– gave his support to the then chair of the Joint Intelligence Committee in interfering with the compilation of a report by the Iraq Survey Group, with the aim of preventing the extent of past mistakes from being made public (section 3.3).

3. The report finds that there is strong evidence that the Prime Minister committed his support to President Bush for an invasion of Iraq in 2002. He did this in the knowledge that the US administration had already decided to oust Saddam Hussein, regardless of any progress on the issue of Iraq's weapons (section 4).

4. The second chapter of the report finds that impeachment proceedings could be begun in order to hold the Prime Minister to account for his misconduct in relation to the Iraq war. It is unprecedented in modern times for a minister to remain in office when faced with such strong evidence of misconduct. All the usual methods of enforcing the authority of Parliament have failed to operate, and therefore, it is necessary to consider what other legal measures are available to Parliament. Authoritative texts on United Kingdom constitutional law describe impeachment as the ultimate means by which Parliament may exercise its legal authority to hold the government to account. Given that impeachment has not been used in recent times, this report provides a brief history of impeachment before considering the grounds for impeaching the Prime Minister.

5. It is for Parliament to decide whether the Prime Minister should be impeached. We consider that this report shows that there is a case of impeachable offences for the Prime Minister to answer.

Chapter I

Statements and actions of the Prime Minister from September 2001 to August 2004 relating to Iraq

6. This chapter details a pattern of seriously misleading statements made by the British Prime Minister, Tony Blair, about Iraq's possession and development of nuclear, biological and chemical (NBC) weapons. It is now clear that these weapons, and therefore the threat they might have posed, did not exist on any substantial scale in the period leading up to the invasion of Iraq in March 2003.

7. As this chapter will demonstrate, the Prime Minister persistently misrepresented, or made statements that were in contrast to, the assessments of the intelligence community. He also made references to statements by the United Nations inspectors which seriously misrepresented those statements. A considerable number of statements made by the Prime Minister about Iraq's weapons were untrue, and there was British intelligence and UN evidence available to the Prime Minister at the time he made these statements showing that they were untrue. The competent exercise of his office would have meant that he knew that what he was saying was unsupported by the facts.

8. Furthermore, evidence that undermined the statements the Prime Minister made concerning Iraqi weapons capabilities and intentions was deliberately concealed from the public and from Members of Parliament, enabling a false case to be presented to the country about Iraq's nuclear, biological and chemical weapons. There is powerful evidence that the persistent misrepresentation about Iraq's NBC weapons occurred because the Prime Minister had, during the course of 2002, committed his support to President Bush for an invasion of Iraq, and that he did this in the knowledge that the US administration had already decided to oust Saddam Hussein, regardless of any progress on the issue of Iraq's weapons.

9. These misrepresentations did not stop with the invasion of Iraq, but have continued in the public statements of the Prime Minister and

his officials on Iraq since then, in their attempts to explain away or obscure the falsity of the claims made by them prior to the invasion.

10. The statements by the Prime Minister were central:
- to the process of highlighting the importance of confronting and threatening the Government of Iraq from late 2001 to early 2003;
- in gaining legal authorisation from the Attorney-General for an invasion of Iraq in February and March 2003;
- in gaining parliamentary support for an invasion of Iraq on 18 March 2003; and
- in justifying the invasion to the electorate in March 2003 and afterwards.

1. The Prime Minister's statements on Iraq's weapons that were unsupported by the intelligence assessments available to him

11. A considerable number of the claims made by the Prime Minister about Iraq's NBC weapons from early 2002 onwards drew upon the authority of the intelligence services for their validation. The Prime Minister purported to have a substantial amount of knowledge, not otherwise in the public realm, which came from this source. This was stated overtly in his presentation to the House of Commons on 24 September 2002:[1]

> 'I am aware, of course, that people are going to have to take elements of this on the good faith of our intelligence services. But *this is what they are telling me* the British Prime Minister and my senior colleagues. The intelligence picture they paint is one accumulated over the past four years. It is extensive, detailed and authoritative.'

12. Nevertheless, a substantial number of the most significant claims made by the Prime Minister were either an exaggeration of intelligence assessments or were in contradiction to intelligence findings that had been reported to him. This misreporting took at least six forms:

1.1 the Prime Minister made claims about the existence of Iraq's weapons that were not backed up by intelligence assessments;

1.2 he made claims about threats from Iraq to the region and the world that were unsubstantiated by intelligence;

1.3 he stated that UN inspectors were reporting that illicit weapons did exist, whilst they were reporting that materials were unaccounted for, even though the distinction between these two categories was drawn clearly in intelligence reports;

1.4 he asserted that Iraq's illicit weapons programme was growing, despite the indications of intelligence that it was not;

1.5 he misreported the findings of the United Nations Monitoring, Verification and Inspection Commission (UNMOVIC) and the International Atomic Energy Agency (IAEA), to portray inspections as futile and to assert that Iraq had committed a 'material breach' of Security Council Resolution 1441; and

1.6 he claimed that material found after April 2003 was part of a covert weapons programme, despite the lack of intelligence to support these claims.

13. These forms of misreporting are described in more detail below.

1.1 Claims made about the existence of Iraq's NBC weapons before intelligence had assessed that Iraq possessed these weapons

14. The Prime Minister made firm claims of certainty about the existence and development of Iraq's NBC weapons from early 2002. On 3 March 2002, he told Australia's Channel Nine:[2]

'We know they are trying to accumulate weapons of mass destruction.'

15. On 11 March 2002, he said at a press conference with US Vice-President Dick Cheney:[3]

'that there is a threat from Saddam Hussein and the weapons of mass destruction that he has acquired is not in doubt at all.'

16. On 3 April 2002, Mr Blair told NBC news:[4]

'We know that he [Saddam Hussein] has stockpiles of major amounts of chemical and biological weapons, we know that he is trying to acquire nuclear capability, we know that he is trying to develop ballistic missile capability of a greater range.'

17. On 6 April 2002, Mr Blair said at a press conference with President Bush:[5]

'There is a reason why weapons inspectors went in there and that is because we know he has been developing these weapons. We know that those weapons constitute a threat.'

18. On 10 April 2002, Mr Blair told the House of Commons:[6]

'Saddam Hussein's regime is despicable, he is developing weapons of mass destruction, and we cannot leave him doing so unchecked. He is a threat to his own people and to the region and, if allowed to develop these weapons, a threat to us also.'

19. These statements were in direct contrast to the intelligence assessments of the Joint Intelligence Committee (JIC) at the time. The latest JIC assessments available to the Prime Minister in March and April 2002 emphasised how little was known about Iraqi NBC programmes, and stopped short of any definitive claims either way on the existence of stockpiles of weapons, or the development of them. The JIC assessment of 15 March 2002 stated:[7]

'Intelligence on Iraq's weapons of mass destruction (WMD) and ballistic missile programmes is sporadic and patchy. [...] From the evidence available to us, we believe Iraq retains some production equipment, and some small stocks of CW agent precursors, and may have hidden small quantities of agents and weapons. [...] There is no intelligence on any BW agent production facilities but one source indicates that Iraq may have developed mobile production facilities.'

20. The discrepancies between intelligence assessments and the statements of the Prime Minister are stark. Whilst the JIC was suggesting that Iraq '***may*** have

hidden *small quantities* of [chemical] agents and weapons', the Prime Minister﹒ was stating that 'we *know* that he has *stockpiles of major amounts* of chemical and biological weapons'.

21. The statements by the Prime Minister themselves provided the context in which intelligence assessments had to be made. The Prime Minister had already declared – without qualification or evidence – that Iraq had prohibited chemical and biological weapons. On 9 September 2002, JIC gave its first assessment that indicated that Iraq had chemical and biological weapons. As the *Review of Intelligence on Weapons of Mass Destruction* ('the Butler report') of 14 July 2004 remarked, the 9 September assessment:

> 'reflected a significant change from previous JIC judgements on Iraqi possession of chemical and biological weapons' (§294).

22. However, this was a change that had been pre-empted by at least six months by the Prime Minister, who had set the tone for the subsequent intelligence assessment.

1.2 Claims about a 'threat' from Iraq's weapons

23. One of the most persistent claims made by the Prime Minister up until the beginning of the invasion in March 2003 was that Iraq constituted a 'threat' to the Middle Eastern region, to the UK and to the world at large.

24. Mr Blair told the House of Commons on 10 April 2002:[8]

> 'there is no doubt at all that the development of weapons of mass destruction by Saddam Hussein *poses a severe threat not just to the region, but to the wider world.* [...] He is a threat to his own people and to the region and, if allowed to develop these weapons, *a threat to us* also.'

25. He told a press conference on 3 September 2002:[9]

> 'Iraq poses a real and a *unique threat to the security of the region and the rest of the world.*'

26. The Prime Minister told the TUC Conference on 10 September 2002:[10]

> 'So let me tell you why I say Saddam Hussein is a threat that has to be dealt with. He has twice before started wars of aggression. Over one million people died in them. When the weapons inspectors were evicted [sic] from Iraq in 1998 there were *still enough chemical and biological weapons remaining to devastate the entire Gulf region.*'

27. In his foreword to *Iraq's Weapons of Mass Destruction: The Assessment of the British Government* of 24 September 2002 ('the September dossier'), the Prime Minister wrote that Iraq was:

> 'a current and serious threat to the UK national interest. [...] I am in no doubt that the threat is serious and current, that he has made progress on WMD, and that he has to be stopped.'

28. The Prime Minister told the House of Commons on 3 February 2003:[11]

> 'Saddam's weapons of mass destruction and the *threats they pose to the world* must be confronted.'

29. On 25 February 2003, he told the House of Commons:[12]

'The intelligence is clear: he [Saddam Hussein] continues to believe his WMD programme is essential both for internal repression and *for external aggression*.'

30. The resolution moved by the Prime Minister in the House of Commons on 18 March 2003, which supported the war on Iraq, included:[13]

'this House [. . .] recognises that Iraq's weapons of mass destruction and long range missiles, and its continuing non-compliance with Security Council Resolutions, pose a threat to international peace and security.'

31. For there to be 'a severe threat [...] to the wider world' from Iraq's NBC weapons, there need to be two distinct components: the capability (the presence of such weapons or their precursor elements, together with a delivery system) and the intention to use these weapons outside its borders. Both components can be, and were, investigated by the British intelligence services, and their reports on their findings were available to the Prime Minister.

32. In direct contrast to the Prime Minister's statements, the intelligence assessments about Iraq throughout the period of 2002-03 make no reference to any intention by Iraq to use NBC weapons outside its borders, either by the Iraqi armed forces or through the supply of such weapons to non-state actors. In fact, the only situation in which the intelligence assessments envisioned that Iraq would use NBC weapons was if Iraq itself was attacked.

33. For example, the interdepartmental advice to ministers in early March 2002, drawing heavily on JIC assessments, stated:[14]

'Saddam has not succeeded in seriously threatening his neighbours. [...] Saddam has used WMD in the past and could do so again if his regime were threatened.'

34. Extensive excerpts of JIC reports have been reprinted or summarised at length in the report of the Intelligence and Security Committee of September 2003 and its Annual Reports of 2002-03 and 2003-04, the documents released during the Hutton inquiry, and the Butler report of July 2004. In these documents, the only discussion of an intention from Iraq to use NBC weapons relates to the analysis of the likely response from Iraq if it were invaded. This was the subject of the JIC paper of 21 August 2002, which was mandated to:[15]

'consider what diplomatic options Saddam has to deter, avert or limit the scope and effectiveness of a US-led attack [and]...his military options for facing a US-led attack.'

35. It was only in this context of a US-led invasion of Iraq that consideration was given to Iraq threatening the use of WMD against other states.[16]

36. The JIC assessment of 9 September 2002, which is otherwise the strongest statement by the JIC of the likelihood of Iraq's possession and development of chemical and biological weapons, stated clearly:[17]

'The use of chemical and biological weapons prior to any military attack would boost support for US-led action and is unlikely.'

37. The assessment of likely Iraqi use of NBC weapons can be found in early drafts of the September dossier by JIC Chair John Scarlett. The 19 September draft referred to only two scenarios in which it envisioned chemical and biological weapons could be used by Iraq: against an internal uprising, and in the following scenario:[18]

'intelligence indicates that Saddam is prepared to use chemical and biological weapons *if he believes his regime is under threat*.'

38. The final clause of this section was omitted from the published version of the dossier, on the urging of Jonathan Powell, the Downing Street chief of staff, on 19 September 2002: this will be discussed further in section 2.4 below.

39. This conclusion is also reached by the Intelligence and Security Committee, which had reviewed JIC assessments:[19]

'Saddam was not considered a current or imminent threat to mainland UK, nor did the dossier say so. As we said in our analysis of the JIC Assessments, the most likely chemical and biological munitions to be used against Western forces were battlefield weapons (artillery and rockets), rather than strategic weapons.'

40. The absence of an assessment that Iraq was intending to use NBC weapons against other countries even without an invasion would have been known to the Prime Minister from JIC assessments. It is also indicated in the first draft of the Prime Minister's foreword to the September dossier, which contained the following sentence:[20]

'The case I make is not that Saddam could launch a nuclear attack on London or another part of the UK (He could not).'

41. This section was omitted from the published version of the foreword: this will be discussed further in section 2.4 below.

42. In addition, it was privately recognised by one of the Prime Minister's closest advisers that the intelligence material did not demonstrate that Iraq was a threat. The Downing Street chief of staff, Jonathan Powell, wrote an email on 17 September 2002 to John Scarlett, about the draft of the September dossier that Scarlett had compiled from intelligence material:[21]

'the document does nothing to demonstrate a threat, let alone an imminent threat from Saddam. In other words it shows he has the means but it does not demonstrate he has the motive to attack his neighbours let alone the west. We will need to make it clear in launching the document that we do not claim that we have evidence that he is an imminent threat.'

43. Despite this note, there was no indication in the final dossier that the UK did not have evidence that Iraq was an imminent threat.

44. Furthermore, the scale of the possible use of Iraqi weapons was greatly exaggerated by the Prime Minister on the basis of the intelligence. The claim to the TUC conference on 10 September 2002 that Iraq had 'enough chemical and biological weapons remaining to devastate the entire Gulf region' is on a

different scale from any JIC assessment, which stated at maximum that Iraq had a capability of up to 20 missiles with a range extending beyond the battlefield. To convert this capacity into a force that could devastate the 'entire Gulf region' – from Kuwait to the straits of Hormuz, comprising 8 countries and 118 million people – would take a remarkable feat of imagination.

45. In summary, there were repeated statements by the Prime Minister in 2002 and 2003 that Iraq constituted a threat to the world and to the UK. The Prime Minister sourced his claim that Iraq sought NBC weapons for the purpose of external aggression to the intelligence services. These statements were in direct contrast to the JIC assessments at the time, which were available to the Prime Minister, and which did not assert that Iraq had the intention to use NBC weapons outside its borders, except in the case of a US-led attack on Iraq. If Iraq was not thought to have had such an intention, it would not constitute the threat as claimed by the Prime Minister.

1.3 Claims that weapons and material that were unaccounted for still existed

46. Throughout the period from 2002-03, the Prime Minister made repeated assertions that any material that the UN weapons inspections of the United Nations Special Commission (UNSCOM) had recorded as unaccounted for, in December 1998 – when the US ordered the inspectors to leave Iraq – still existed.

47. Up to 1998, a substantial part of the work of the weapons inspectors in Iraq was to discover what had happened to the chemical and biological agents that Iraq had produced before their entry in 1991, and to check the documentation that showed how much of each agent Iraq had manufactured. However, the amount of agent Iraq is thought to have produced before 1991 was itself uncertain. UNSCOM calculated the maximum amounts that Iraq could have produced from the biological growth media or the chemical precursors, and subtracted from this total the amount Iraq could prove not to have produced, used in its wars against Iran and the Kurdish population, destroyed unilaterally, or presented to UNSCOM for destruction. The total left over – which could not be demonstrated to have been unmanufactured, used or disposed of – was recorded as 'unaccounted for'.

48. The levels of agents that were unaccounted for in this way were large. However, the fact that these quantities of actual and potential production were unaccounted for did not mean that they still existed. Iraq was unable to prove that it had used specific quantities of chemical weapons against Iran in the 1980-88 war; it had also destroyed large quantities of its own stocks of these weapons in 1991 without keeping sufficient proof of its actions. In the case of the growth media anthrax, for example, UNSCOM 'confirmed that [growth] media was burnt and buried there [at al-Hakam, the former production facility] [in 1991] but the types and quantities are not known'.[22] It thus recorded the entire quantity of growth media as still unaccounted for in its final substantive report of January 1999.

49. In some cases, it is quite clear that any stocks that were retained no longer exist in usable form. Most chemical and biological agents are subject to

processes of deterioration; botulinum toxin, aflatoxin and chemical G-agents (sarin, tabun and cyclosarin) all deteriorate fairly rapidly.

50. These considerations were ignored by the Prime Minister in his speeches that mentioned material that was unaccounted for. For example, he told the TUC conference on 10 September 2002:[23]

> 'When the weapons inspectors were evicted [sic] from Iraq in 1998 there were still enough chemical and biological weapons remaining to devastate the entire Gulf region.'

51. He told the House of Commons on 25 February 2003:[24]

> 'Is it not reasonable that Saddam provides evidence of destruction of the biological and chemical agents and weapons *the UN proved he had* in 1999? So far he has provided none.'

52. He told the House of Commons on 18 March 2003, in the debate that led to a vote to support the invasion of Iraq:[25]

> 'When the inspectors left in 1998, they left unaccounted for 10 thousand litres of anthrax; a far reaching VX nerve agent programme; up to 6,500 chemical munitions; at least 80 tonnes of mustard gas, possibly more than ten times that amount; unquantifiable amounts of sarin, botulinum toxin and a host of other biological poisons; an entire Scud missile programme. We are now seriously asked to accept that in the last few years, contrary to all history, contrary to all intelligence, he decided unilaterally to destroy *the weapons*. Such a claim is palpably absurd.'

53. These three claims all rely upon the direct assumption that material that was unaccounted for by UNSCOM in 1998 still in fact existed. By contrast, UNSCOM and their successors in UNMOVIC repeatedly drew the distinction between what was unaccounted for and what was known to exist. For example, UNMOVIC executive chairman Hans Blix told the UN Security Council on 14 February 2003:[26]

> 'many proscribed weapons and items are not accounted for. To take an example, a document, which Iraq provided, suggested to us that some 1,000 tonnes of chemical agent were 'unaccounted for'. *One must not jump to the conclusion that they exist.*'

54. Furthermore, JIC assessments throughout the period made it clear that the quantity of material unaccounted for in December 1998 was not to be taken as indicating extant stockpiles. This was why JIC assessments repeatedly considered the possibility that the Iraqi government had only small amounts of chemical and biological agent, and that the quantities unaccounted for (referred to as 'anomalies' here) suggest possibilities not certainties:[27]

> 'From the evidence available to us, we believe Iraq [...] may have hidden small quantities of agents and weapons. Anomalies in Iraqi declarations to UNSCOM *suggest* stocks could be much larger.'

55. Despite frequent reminders from UNMOVIC and JIC that material which was unaccounted for could not be automatically considered as still existing, the Prime Minister repeatedly conflated the two categories. As a result, he was able to portray Iraq as holding substantial stockpiles of chemical and biological weapons, despite the indications from the weapons inspectors to the contrary.

1.4 Claims of an escalating NBC programme

56. The claims made by the Prime Minister about Iraq's weapons acquired a sense of urgency by his assertions of how the Iraqi programme to produce NBC weapons was escalating.

57. On 16 July 2002, the Prime Minister told the House of Commons Liaison Committee:[28]

'as more negotiations go on and he fails to comply and you know that he is developing these weapons of mass destruction, then over a period of time you are entitled to draw the conclusion that *this threat is growing not diminishing*.'

58. On 10 September 2002, he told the TUC conference that Saddam Hussein was making a huge annual investment in his illicit weapons programmes:[29]

'He now gets around $3 billion through illicit trading every year. It is unaccounted for, but almost certainly used for his weapons programmes.'

59. On 24 September 2002, he told the House of Commons:[30]

'The reason [for the publication of the September dossier] is because his chemical, biological and nuclear weapons programme is not an historic leftover from 1998. The inspectors aren't needed to clean up the old remains. His WMD programme is *active, detailed and growing*. The policy of containment is not working. The WMD programme is not shut down. It is up and running.'

60. The Prime Minister's foreword to the dossier itself asserted:

'The picture presented to me by the JIC in recent months has become more not less worrying.'

61. These statements were in contrast to the reports of the intelligence services, which – despite strengthening in their assessment that Iraq had chemical and biological weapons from September 2002 – did not argue that the NBC programmes themselves were escalating. Interdepartmental advice to ministers in early March 2002, drawing heavily on JIC assessments, concluded with the following judgements:[31]
– 'Sanctions have effectively frozen Iraq's nuclear programme;
  – Iraq has been prevented from rebuilding its chemical arsenal to pre-Gulf War levels;
  – Ballistic missile programmes have been severely restricted;
  – Biological weapons (BW) and Chemical Weapons (CW) programmes have been hindered'

62. The Butler report assessed this interdepartmental advice was 'a fair and balanced summary of the most recent JIC assessments.' (§262)

63. The position of the intelligence services throughout the period from early 2002 until March 2003 is summarised in the Butler report (§427):

> 'The Government's conclusion in the spring of 2002 that stronger action (although not necessarily military action) needed to be taken to enforce Iraqi disarmament was not based on any new development in the current intelligence picture on Iraq. In his evidence to us, the Prime Minister endorsed the view expressed at the time that what had changed was not the pace of Iraq's prohibited weapons programmes, which had not been dramatically stepped up, but tolerance of them following the attacks of 11 September 2001. [...] there was no recent intelligence that would itself have given rise to a conclusion that Iraq was of more immediate concern than the activities of some other countries.'

64. In summary, the Prime Minister had declared in September 2002 that the reason for producing the dossier at the time was that Iraq's NBC programme was 'growing'. This was in contrast to the intelligence assessment that Iraq's illicit programme had been frozen or hindered, and to the fact that there was no intelligence of a growing programme. The Prime Minister has now recognised that the cause for concern was not a growing programme, but a changed political environment, which is a direct contradiction of his statement of 24 September 2002.

1.5 Claims about the work of UNMOVIC and the IAEA and the 'material breach' of Security Council Resolution 1441

65. Weapons inspections resumed on 27 November 2002, and were conducted by UNMOVIC and the IAEA. The Prime Minister, however, judged that they were not being successful in disarming Iraq of illicit weapons. He argued that this meant that Iraq had committed a 'material breach' of Security Council Resolution 1441, and this reactivated the authorisation to use force in Security Council Resolution 678 (1990). It was on this basis that he concurred in the termination of weapons inspections and the commencement of the invasion in March 2003.

66. **This report does not review the full legal case about the invasion, and does not endorse the view that the UK has the right to unilaterally enforce Security Council Resolutions.** It does however take note of the opinion that the Attorney-General transmitted to the Prime Minister. In the summary provided by the Butler report (§379), this advice was that, for the invasion of Iraq to be lawful:

> 'It did, however, require the Prime Minister, in the absence of a further United Nations Security Council resolution, to be satisfied that there were strong factual grounds for concluding that Iraq had failed to take the final opportunity to comply with its disarmament obligations under relevant resolutions of the Security Council and that *it was possible to demonstrate hard evidence of non-compliance and non-co-operation with the requirements of Security Council Resolution 1441*, so as to justify the conclusion that Iraq was in further material breach of its obligations.'

67. The Prime Minister's Private Secretary wrote to the Legal Secretary of the Attorney-General on 15 March 2003:[32]

'it is indeed the Prime Minister's unequivocal view that Iraq is in further material breach of its obligations, as in OP4 18 of UNSCR 1441, because of 'false statements or omissions in the declarations submitted by Iraq pursuant to this resolution and failure by Iraq to comply with, and co-operate fully in the implementation of, this resolution'.

68. Thus, it was the Prime Minister's position on 15 March 2003 that he had evidence that Iraq was not complying with the terms of Security Council Resolution 1441. For this reason, this section examines the chief allegations made by the Prime Minister at the time of Iraq's 'non-compliance and non-co-operation', as this provided the basis of the Prime Minister's claim to be acting lawfully in ordering the invasion of Iraq. It evaluates whether these allegations were compatible with the reports made by UNMOVIC and the IAEA at this time.

69. The Prime Minister stated on 25 February 2003:[33]

'After 12 years is it not reasonable that the UN inspectors have unrestricted access to Iraqi scientists – that means no tape recorders, no minders, no intimidation, interviews outside Iraq as provided for by Resolution 1441? So far *this simply isn't happening*.'

70. By indicating that *no* interviews were happening in private, the Prime Minister was making a clear misstatement of the information provided by the weapons inspectors themselves. Dr Mohamed El Baradei, the director general of the IAEA, told the Security Council on 14 February 2003 – eleven days before the Prime Minister's statement:[34]

'The IAEA has continued to interview key Iraqi personnel. We have recently been able to conduct *four interviews in private* – that is, without the presence of an Iraqi observer. The interviewees, however, have tape recorded their interviews. [. . .] I should note that, during our recent meeting in Baghdad, Iraq reconfirmed its commitment to encourage its citizens to accept interviews in private, both inside and outside of Iraq.'

71. Similarly, UNMOVIC executive chairman Hans Blix recorded at the Security Council on the same day:[35]

'Three persons that had previously refused interviews on UNMOVIC's terms, subsequently *accepted such interviews* just prior to our talks in Baghdad on 8 and 9 February. These interviews proved informative.'

72. No interviews were held out of the country simply because neither the IAEA nor UNMOVIC had yet requested any interviews to be held out of the country. On 7 March 2003, Dr Blix announced that he was intending to begin requests of interviews outside the country. The invasion began before he had the opportunity to make such requests. His report to the Security Council on that day also makes the extent of the mistake in the Prime Minister's statement clear:[36]

'While *the Iraqi side seems to have encouraged interviewees not to request the presence of Iraqi officials (so-called minders) or the taping of the interviews*, conditions ensuring the absence of undue influences are difficult to attain inside Iraq.

Interviews outside the country might provide such assurance. It is our intention to request such interviews shortly. Nevertheless, despite remaining shortcomings, interviews are useful. Since we started requesting interviews, 38 individuals were asked for private interviews, of which 10 accepted under our terms, 7 of these during the last week.'

73. The Prime Minister said on 25 February 2003:[37]

'Is it not reasonable that Saddam provides evidence of destruction of the biological and chemical agents and weapons the UN proved he had in 1999? So far he has provided none.'

74. The claim that the 'UN proved' that Iraq had chemical and biological agents in 1999 is dealt with in section 1.3 above. However, the assertion that no evidence had been provided for the prior destruction of chemical and biological agents is *in direct contradiction with the accounts of the inspectors themselves*.

75. With regard to biological agents, on 19 February 2003, Iraq invited UNMOVIC to excavate al-Aziziya Range (100km southwest of Baghdad), the site of the purported destruction of bombs that had been filled with biological agents, claiming that the material was no longer so dangerous.[38] It was visited by UNMOVIC's biological team from 24 February. In the news update of 26 February 2003, UNMOVIC gave the following description:[39]

'An UNMOVIC biological team returned to the Al Aziziyah Range, where excavations of the R400 aerial bombs were under way. Iraq claims that these bombs filled with biological agents had been unilaterally destroyed in 1991. The team observed the excavation of a pit and inspected excavated munitions and fragments. UNMOVIC also conducted an aerial survey of the site.'

76. On both 27 and 28 February, 'Additional fragments of R-400 bombs were identified' (similarly, on 2 and 3 March).[40] The contents of these bomb fragments were subject to analysis from 2 March 2003. A full account was provided by Hans Blix in his 7 March 2003 statement to the Security Council:[41]

'To date, Iraq has unearthed eight complete bombs comprising two liquid-filled intact R-400 bombs and six other complete bombs. Bomb fragments were also found. Samples have been taken. The investigation of the destruction site could, in the best case, allow the determination of the number of bombs destroyed at that site. It should be followed by a serious and credible effort to determine the separate issue of how many R-400 type bombs were produced. In this, as in other matters, inspection work is moving on and may yield results.'

77. On chemical agents, Iraq provided the 6-page 'Air Force' document (which had been discovered at Iraqi Air Force headquarters in July 1998) to UNMOVIC on 30 November 2002, in an attempt to clarify the amount of chemical weapons used in the Iran-Iraq war.[42] This was a key demand of UNMOVIC in order to ascertain how much chemical agent was unaccounted for. It was recorded as still being under review by UNMOVIC in its 6 March 2003 report.[43]

78. Furthermore, UNMOVIC recorded progress on 19 December 2002 in accounting for chemical warfare precursors, with information provided by Iraq. Hans Blix told the Security Council:[44]

'In the chemical weapons field, Iraq has further explained its account of the material balance of precursors for chemical warfare agents. Although it does not resolve outstanding issues on this subject, it may help to achieve a better understanding of the fate of the precursors.'

79. Thus, to take these examples, it is clear from the accounts of the UN inspectors before the Prime Minister's statement that Iraq was providing evidence of the destruction of chemical and biological warfare agents that were unaccounted for in 1999. The statement from the Prime Minister is in direct contradiction to the account of the weapons inspectors.

80. In his speech at the Azores summit on 16 March 2003, the Prime Minister repeated the misleading allegation that no interviews had taken place outside of Iraq, as his first allegation to buttress his claim that Iraq was in violation of Security Council Resolution 1441.[45] The second allegation listed by the Prime Minister in this speech to support this claim was as follows:

'Still no proper production or evidence of the destruction of, just to take one example, the ten thousand litres of anthrax that the inspectors just a week ago said was unaccounted for.'

81. This claim was in direct contradiction with the account of the UN weapons inspectors.

82. Since February 2003, the Iraqi government had been providing documentation to demonstrate its claim that it destroyed its anthrax stocks in 1991. An account was provided by Hans Blix in his 7 March 2003 statement to the Security Council:[46]

'More papers on anthrax [. . .] have recently been provided. [. . .] Iraq proposed an investigation using advanced technology to quantify the amount of unilaterally destroyed anthrax dumped at a site.'

83. This was nine days before the Prime Minister delivered his speech, but was ignored by him in claiming that Iraq was providing no evidence. The details of the Iraqi programme to account for past anthrax destruction was described at length in UNMOVIC's report of 30 May 2003. UNMOVIC recorded that the new information did not conclusively prove that Iraq had destroyed all its anthrax, but it recorded notable progress:[47]

'While the Iraqi side continued to claim that no documentary evidence remained of the destruction operation, it took two different steps in an effort to prove its declaration that all had been destroyed. As described in the present report, the Iraqi side undertook a chemical analysis of soil samples from the site where a quantity of anthrax was declared to have been dumped in 1991. While the results of the analysis were consistent with the declaration that anthrax had been dumped at the site, the study could not provide evidence of the quantities destroyed. The other step taken by the Iraqi side was to supply lists of the persons who in 1991 had been engaged in the operations to destroy anthrax. [. . .]

On 26 February 2003, Iraq submitted a report describing a study it had initiated to try and show, through scientific means, that it had indeed disposed of chemically inactivated *B. anthracis* (anthrax) agent, in the quantity it had declared, at the Al Hakam dump site in 1991.

On 1 March 2003, UNMOVIC and Iraqi experts discussed the report and the preliminary results of the analysis of soil from the dump site. On 19 March 2003, Iraq submitted another paper with more analytical results and indicated that it would attempt to perform a qualitative and quantitative chemical and biological analysis of soil samples taken in a defined grid pattern from an area of the dump site that had been identified by UNSCOM in 1996. In support, Iraq also provided a report on the geophysical characteristics of the sampling area. Given that 12 years had elapsed since the material was stated to have been disposed of, such information would be essential to properly interpret the analytical results.'

84. For the Prime Minister to dismiss this progress as 'no proper [...] evidence of the destruction of [...] anthrax' is to wholly misrepresent the work of the UN inspectors.

85. The most serious misrepresentations of the work of the UN inspectors occurred in the Prime Minister's statement to the House of Commons on 18 March 2003. In this speech he moved the motion that was adopted by the House of Commons in giving its support to an invasion of Iraq. His claims about Iraq's non-compliance with UN inspectors began:[48]

'On 7 March, the inspectors published a remarkable document. It is 173 pages long, and details all the unanswered questions about Iraq's weapons of mass destruction. It lists 29 different areas in which the inspectors have been unable to obtain information.'

86. This is a direct misrepresentation of the 'Clusters document' issued by UNMOVIC on 7 March 2003. It was not about '29 different areas in which the inspectors have been unable to obtain information', but an overview of the 29 different areas on which UNMOVIC sought further information. For example, to take the topic of mycotoxins (aflatoxin and trichothecenes), one of the 29 areas (and one highlighted by the Prime Minister in the September dossier), UNMOVIC reviewed the information provided to it by Iraq, and assessed:[49]

'UNMOVIC concludes that the development of the agent [trichothecene] did not proceed much beyond the research and laboratory stage [...] stocks [of aflatoxin] would have degraded and would contain little if any viable agent in 2003.'

87. It still requested some further information from Iraq – in clarifying the process that led to the decision to produce aflatoxin, detailing the number of munitions filled with it before 1991, and in providing laboratory notes on mycotoxin. However, to state, as the Prime Minister did, that 'the inspectors have been unable to obtain information' on Iraq's past mycotoxin programme is to contradict the substance of the inspectors' report.

88. The first case presented in this speech by the Prime Minister to justify his assertion that the Clusters document demonstrated Iraqi non-compliance was:

'On VX, for example, it says: "Documentation available to UNMOVIC suggests that Iraq at least had had far reaching plans to weaponise VX".'

89. This quotation, from p.84 of the Clusters document, was in a section marked 'Background' about the history of Iraq's programmes, and was *about Iraqi intentions in 1988*. This was not mentioned by the Prime Minister, who gave the mistaken impression through his highly selective quotation that UNMOVIC was referring to current Iraqi plans.

90. By contrast, the actual account by UNMOVIC in the 'assessment' section of the report was that Iraq used two different methods of producing VX, called 'route B' and 'route D'. This was UNMOVIC's assessment of Iraq's VX:[50]

'VX produced through route B must be used relatively quickly after production (about 1 to 8 weeks) [. . .]

Based upon the documents provided by Iraq, it is doubtful that any significant quantities of VX were produced using [route D] before the Gulf war.'

91. Although questions remained about precursor chemicals for VX, for the Prime Minister to leave his audience with the strong impression that the UN was recording current Iraqi plans to weaponise VX is to directly misrepresent the UNMOVIC report. The UN report recorded that any VX produced by the first of the two methods Iraq had developed would have long decomposed; and that it was unlikely that Iraq had produced significant quantities of VX using the second method. The opposite interpretation of the UN report was given by the Prime Minister in his statement of 18 March 2003.

92. Hans Blix provided an overall summary of the extent of Iraq cooperation with the UN inspectors to the Security Council on 7 March 2003: [51]

'the numerous initiatives, which are now taken by the Iraqi side with a view to resolving some long-standing open disarmament issues, *can be seen as "active", or even "proactive"*'.

93. In summary, the allegations made by the Prime Minister in the House of Commons on 18 March 2003 resort to direct misrepresentation of the reports of UN inspectors in order to make the case that Iraq was in material breach of Security Council Resolution 1441. The Prime Minister thus did not fulfil the requirement laid down by the Attorney-General that he make sure there were strong factual grounds for concluding that Iraq was not complying or cooperating with its obligations. In presenting what he had been told by the Attorney-General was crucial evidence for the invasion to be lawful, the Prime Minister resorted to exaggeration, misquotation and fabrication.

1.6 Claims made about items found in Iraq after April 2003

94. The Prime Minister indicated during the invasion process that he firmly believed that NBC weapons would be found by Coalition personnel within a short timeframe. He said on 8 April 2003:[52]

'On weapons of mass destruction, we know that the regime has them, we know that as the regime collapses we will be led to them.'

95. Iraq did not use NBC weapons during the invasion, and no such weapons were immediately discovered. However, some items that were found were subjected to further analysis in the suspicion that these items might be facilities involved in the production of chemical and biological weapons.

96. On 30 May 2003, the Prime Minister asserted:[53]

'We have already found two trailers, both of which we believe were used for the production of biological weapons [. . .]'

97. On 2 June 2003, the Prime Minister claimed again:[54]

'I would point out to you, we already have, according to our experts, two mobile biological weapons facilities that were almost certainly part, according to our intelligence, of a whole set of those facilities.'

98. It emerged subsequently that these trailers were not suitable for the production of biological weapons, and had been constructed for other purposes.[55] Moreover, the Prime Minister's assertion appears to have pre-empted the assessment of the trailers by British intelligence.

99. It was only on 5 June, a week later, that a British weapons expert, David Kelly, arrived to inspect the trailers, and concluded that the trailers were not for the production of biological weapons. According to Bryan Wells, the director of counter proliferation and arms control at the Ministry of Defence whom Kelly advised, Kelly 'was of the view that these were not biological weapons facilities', and that he was the only British official to inspect the trailers who reported back to him.[56] Kelly himself confirmed this in an email of 11 June 2003.[57]

100. Therefore, the Prime Minister had stated a collective belief ('**we** believe' and 'according to **our** experts') that the trailers were used for biological weapons production prior to any investigation of those trailers by intelligence experts. He was thus misrepresenting the position of the intelligence assessment by neither waiting for it nor withdrawing his own statement when the intelligence findings had been circulated.

101. The Prime Minister also undertook to publicise his interpretation of the findings of the Iraq Survey Group, the US-led inspections body, to support his earlier position. On 16 December 2003, he told the British Forces Broadcasting Service:[58]

'the Iraq Survey Group has already found massive evidence of a *huge system of clandestine laboratories* [. . .]. Now frankly these things weren't being developed unless they were developed for a purpose.'

102. The Prime Minister's spokesperson clarified that this statement was based upon the interim report of the Iraq Survey Group, published on 2 October

2003, and not upon secret intelligence.[59] That report had referred to:[60]

> 'A clandestine network of laboratories and safehouses within the Iraqi Intelligence Service that contained equipment subject to UN monitoring and suitable for continuing CBW research.'

103. That is, the report did not claim there was a 'huge system', and comes to no conclusion about what purpose the laboratories had. Later in the report, it recorded that investigations were ongoing. *The Prime Minister's account of the findings of the report was thus a significant exaggeration of what the report itself stated.*

2. Failure to disclose available counter-evidence, and to ensure claims were verified

104. The government, including the Prime Minister, has been in possession of a substantial amount of information that undermined the case that it was presenting to the public about Iraq's weapons, but which it chose not to disclose. In consequence, Members of Parliament and the public were unable to make a properly informed judgement of the scale of the threat posed by Iraq at the time they were asked by the government to support the invasion. The retention of information has also prevented the government and the Prime Minister from being adequately exposed to properly informed criticism after the invasion.

105. Naturally, much intelligence information cannot be released for security reasons, but it is difficult to see how not disclosing the information detailed below could be justified in this way. Instead, this material strongly indicates that the Prime Minister and his officials held back material that would have substantiated the viewpoint that Iraq was not a serious threat, particularly in comparison with other potential threats to the UK, and did not have a substantial programme to develop or stockpile NBC weapons.

2.1 Sources who gave a different account

106. The most prominent defector from Iraq was Hussein Kamel, Saddam Hussein's son-in-law and director of Iraq's Military Industrialization Corporation, who had been in charge of Iraq's weapons programme throughout the 1980s and first half of the 1990s. After he defected to Jordan on 7 August 1995, Hussein Kamel told UN inspectors 'I ordered the destruction of all chemical weapons. *All weapons – biological, chemical, missile, nuclear were destroyed'.*[61]

107. The Butler report confirms that this claim was known to the British intelligence services. The JIC reported on 24 August 1995 that: 'Hussein Kamel claims there are no remaining stockpiles of agent' (§177). However, this information was not released to the public throughout this period. Instead, the Prime Minister repeatedly referred to Hussein Kamel's defection in order to support his case that the Iraqi regime had retained stockpiles of chemical and

biological weapons and was developing more of these weapons.

108. For example, on 25 February 2003, the Prime Minister told the House of Commons:[62]

'It was only four years later after the defection of Saddam's son-in-law to Jordan, that the offensive biological weapons and the full extent of the nuclear programme were discovered. In all, 17 UN Resolutions were passed. None was obeyed. At no stage did he co-operate.'

109. In fact, Hussein Kamel had told the UN inspectors that Iraq had cooperated with the UN Security Council Resolution insofar as it did not hold stockpiles of NBC weapons any longer.

110. On 18 February 2003, the Prime Minister told a Downing Street press conference:[63]

'And I would just draw attention once again to the biological weapons programme that he absolutely categorically denied existed, said it was all a fabrication of the CIA and the British intelligence services, and then when his son-in-law defected to Jordan and admitted that they had an offensive biological weapons programme, the Iraqis then co-operated, and then of course they were able, at least partially, *to shut the programme down.*'

111. Similarly, he wrote in the *Independent on Sunday* on 2 March 2003:[64]

'The UN inspectors found no trace at all of Saddam's offensive biological weapons programme – which he claimed didn't exist – until his lies were revealed by his son-in-law. *Only then did the inspectors find over 8,000 litres of concentrated anthrax* and other biological weapons, and a factory to make more.'

112. In fact, Iraq had admitted a biological weapons research programme in 1992, and had admitted an offensive biological weapons programme, including the production of biological agents, on 1 July 1995, before the defection of Hussein Kamel.[65] Furthermore, the weapons inspectors did not 'shut the programme down' as a result of Hussein Kamel's defection: as Kamel revealed to the inspectors, the programme had already been shut down over four years earlier.

113. One can only assume that this information was made up by the Prime Minister as inspectors never found live anthrax in Iraq, and the factory at which anthrax had been produced before 1991 was under UN monitoring from at least October 1991.[66] And, most importantly, the Prime Minister's indication that Iraq still had biological weapons in 1995 was in direct contrast to the statement of Hussein Kamel himself.

114. However, it was not possible for observers to understand the flaws in the Prime Minister's case, because Kamel's own account was not known at this time in the UK other than to the government itself. It was only when the transcript of Kamel's interview was leaked to two academics on 26 February 2003 that the extent of his prior claims was known.

115. There has been no explanation of why this information was held back by the government. There was no danger to anyone from releasing this information, as Kamel had already been killed in 1996. It is reasonable to conclude that the

nature of Kamel's claims was not released to the public and to Parliament because his assertions undermined the government's allegations that Iraq had retained an extensive stockpile of prohibited weapons.

116. Similarly, the Butler report recorded that two sources 'regarded as reliable' by the intelligence services 'tended to present a less worrying view of Iraqi chemical and biological weapons capability' (§404). The decision to favour those sources with alarmist perspectives over those who presented a 'less worrying view' is not supported by any operational or security consideration. *The reasonable conclusion is that it was a political choice to exaggerate the scale of the threat Iraq posed.*

2.2 Investigation of intelligence sources

117. The Butler report demonstrated how a considerable number of sources or claims of dubious reliability but of a highly alarming nature were not evaluated thoroughly. It explained the lack of checks upon sources by pointing to how the relevant staff – 'Requirements' officers, in the jargon – were 'junior officers', who were in those positions 'in order to make overall staff savings' (§414).

118. However, the failure to investigate properly the claims of alarming sources on such a crucial issue reflects a lack of political priority in evaluating these claims with appropriate scepticism. It is difficult to imagine that if Mr Blair had seriously pressed MI6 or JIC about how reliable their information sources were, it would have been left to 'junior officers' to make all the checks on reliability. Two key examples recounted by the Butler report are as follows.

119. **Uranium from Niger.** The basis of the government's case, according to the Butler report, was: 'During 2002, the UK received further intelligence from additional sources which identified the purpose of [an Iraqi official's] visit to Niger as having been to negotiate the purchase of uranium ore' (§495).

120. Although these 'additional sources' are not described in the Butler report, one of them was not the Iraqi official at the centre of the allegations – Ambassador Wissam al-Zahawi, referred to in the Butler report at §502. After he retired from Iraqi government service in 2001, Zahawi was resident in Amman, Jordan (where there is also a large MI6 station) and paid a number of visits to the UK in 2001 and 2002. At no point did British officials contact him to discuss his trip to Niger, even though the news media had named him in 1999 as the official visiting Niger. His contact details, including his telephone number and email address, were readily available from a reputable academic database. He was contacted by the International Atomic Energy Agency after the September dossier had been published, and was interviewed by them in February 2003. However, at no point did the British intelligence services make contact with him.

121. The failure of the intelligence services to contact Zahawi on an issue so crucial as to be key evidence for whether or not Iraq had an ongoing nuclear programme reflects not just on the junior nature of the staff. It also raises the issue of whether questions were not asked because no one was interested in answers that would not support the presumption of Iraq's active nuclear

ambitions. It demonstrates the political inexpediency of making a serious attempt to investigate alarming allegations about Iraq for their actual plausibility.

122. The doubtful nature of the claims made about Iraq's attempts to purchase uranium from Niger should have been particularly apparent given the reluctance from the United States to endorse those claims. The CIA's director of the Weapons, Intelligence, Non-Proliferation and Arms Control Centre (WINPAC) told the Senate Intelligence Committee that the CIA had urged Britain to remove references to the uranium claim from the September dossier.[67] Although the British government has claimed to have two sources separate to those of the US about Zahawi's visit to Niger in 1999, the suspicion raised by the CIA should have made the British government more vigilant about checking available sources than they were, if it was truly concerned about the possibility of an Iraqi nuclear programme.

123. **Deployment of chemical and biological weapons within 45 minutes**. The Butler report demonstrates that the British intelligence services mentioned that the sub-source who provided the information that Iraq could use CBW of some sort within 45 minutes had 'links to opposition groups and the possibility that his reports would be affected by that.' (§403; this is the individual referred to as the sub-source for the 45 minutes claims at §512). This opposition group referred to seems to be the Iraqi National Accord (INA), led by interim Prime Minister Iyad Allawi, according to the INA's own statements.[68] As a result, there was a clear incentive for the individual source to make alarming claims to British intelligence officials and their conduits.

124. The Butler report mentions that 'post-war validation by SIS has raised serious doubts about the reliability of reporting from this new sub-source' (§403). There seems to have been every possibility that further attempts to assess the reliability of the sub-source could have been made prior to incorporating his claim in such a categorical way into the September 2002 dossier. If it were the case that circumstances rendered it impossible to ascertain his reliability, then it would seem proper that the dubious provenance of the source – as well as the nature of the claim, relating to battlefield weapons – should have been made public.

2.3 Limitations of intelligence sources

125. The Prime Minister presented the intelligence sources available to him as overwhelming and decisive. He told the BBC on 21 April 2002:[69]

'The evidence of Saddam Hussein on weapons of mass destruction is vast.'

126. The Prime Minister told Parliament in releasing the September dossier on 24 September 2002:

'The intelligence picture they [the intelligence services] paint is one accumulated over the past four years. It is *extensive, detailed and authoritative*. [. . .]

'with this accumulated, *detailed intelligence* available; with what we know and what we can reasonably speculate: would the world be wise to leave the present situation undisturbed [. . .]?'

127. The Butler report demonstrated that these assertions were misleading on two grounds: the number of human intelligence sources was very limited, and that excessive reliability was placed on sources of unproven reliability. According to the Butler report (§355), over four-fifths of the intelligence about Iraqi deception and concealment activities came from only two sources. Two-thirds of the total amount of intelligence on this theme came from just one individual. Both of these sources are now recognised as being of questionable reliability. On Iraqi weapons, two-thirds of all intelligence reports that were circulated in 2002 came from just two sources (§401): one reported only indirectly, and the validity of the other is now open to 'serious doubt' (§403).

128. The Butler report also recorded (§406) that the 'vast majority of the intelligence' on Iraqi purported mobile biological capacity came from just one individual (presumably, 'Curveball', the individual associated with the Iraqi National Congress, held by Germany's Federal Intelligence Service),[70] with whom no British official had even met prior to the war. None of this information was disclosed to the public by the government, even though it would have enabled the public to make a much better assessment of the reliability of the intelligence claims.

129. In total, therefore, the considerable majority of British intelligence on Iraq beyond what was already in the public realm came from just five individuals. It is in this regard that the Butler report remarked (§304):

'we were struck by the relative thinness of the intelligence base supporting the greater firmness of the JIC's judgements on Iraqi production and possession of chemical and biological weapons'.

130. This information was not conveyed in any presentation by the Prime Minister or his officials, and was directly misrepresented in some statements. For example, the September dossier alleges that the information about mobile biological laboratories is based upon 'evidence from defectors [which] has indicated the existence of such facilities'. Given that the 'vast majority' of the claims came from just one individual, the claim that 'defectors' (in the plural) were responsible for the evidence was simply misleading.

131. Furthermore, concerns were raised about the reliability of the information coming from these sources. According to the Butler report (§403), the second of the two sources on Iraq's weapons was reporting 'a new sub-source on Iraqi chemical and biological programmes and intentions'. The intelligence reports on this sub-source:

'properly included a caution about the sub-source's links to opposition groups and the possibility that his reports would be affected by that. We have been told that post-war validation by SIS has raised serious doubts about the reliability of reporting from this new sub-source.'

132. Despite these doubts, the Butler report recorded (§401) that the report from this sub-source 'had a major effect on the certainty of statements in the Government's dossier of September 2002 that Iraq possessed and was producing

chemical and biological weapons.' This sub-source was thus crucial to the allegations made about Iraq, despite the concerns raised at the time about his or her reliability.

133. Similarly, on 11 September 2002, a report from a 'new source on trial' was issued which, according to the Butler report (§405) 'did provide significant assurance to those drafting the Government's dossier that active, current production of chemical and biological agent was taking place.' However, this source was unproven, and the report was withdrawn in July 2003 (see section 3.2 below).

134. *The Prime Minister was aware of the limitations of the sources.* The Butler report recorded (§578):

> As it happened, the Chief of SIS had a meeting with the Prime Minister on 12 September to brief him on SIS operations in respect of Iraq. At this meeting, *he briefed the Prime Minister on each of SIS's main sources* including the new source on trial. He told us that he had underlined to the Prime Minister the potential importance of the new source and what SIS understood his access to be; but also said that *the case was developmental and that the source remained unproven.*

135. Despite these concerns, the Prime Minister expressed certainty about the existence of Iraq's weapons and spoke of the evidence as 'authoritative'. This was a clear case of misleading the public and Parliament about the reliability of the evidence.

2.4 Assessment that Iraq would not use weapons outside its own territory unless attacked

136. Assessments of the Joint Intelligence Committee in 2002 considered in detail the circumstances in which Iraq might use any chemical or biological weapons that it might possess.

137. The interdepartmental advice to ministers in early March 2002, drawing heavily on JIC assessments, stated:[71]

> 'Saddam has used WMD in the past and could do so again *if his regime were threatened.*'

138. The JIC assessment of 9 September 2002 was compiled in order to assess possible scenarios in which Iraq might use chemical and biological weapons. It stated in its 'key judgements':[72]

> 'The use of chemical and biological weapons prior to any military attack would boost support for US-led action and *is unlikely.*'

139. The main text of the JIC assessment stated:[73]

> 'One report states that Saddam would not use CBW during the initial air phase of any military campaign but would use CBW once a ground invasion of Iraq has begun. Faced with the likelihood of military defeat and being removed from power, we judge that it is unlikely there would be any way to deter Saddam from using CBW.'

140. The assessment considers the possibility that Iraq might use chemical and biological weapons preemptively, but concludes:[74]

'On balance however we judge that the political cost of using CBW weapons would outweigh the military advantages and that *Saddam would probably not use CBW weapons preemptively.*'

141. This JIC assessment from 9 September 2002 also stated:[75]

'there is no intelligence to indicate that Iraq has considered using chemical and biological agents in terrorist attacks'

142. The same assessment of likely Iraqi use of NBC weapons was found in early drafts of the September dossier by JIC Chair John Scarlett. The 19 September draft referred to only two scenarios in which it envisioned chemical and biological weapons could be used by Iraq: against an internal uprising, and in the following scenario:[76]

'intelligence indicates that Saddam is prepared to use chemical and biological weapons *if he believes his regime is under threat.*'

143. *The consistent view of the intelligence services, as reported to the Prime Minister, over the period from March to September 2002, was that Iraq would be likely to use chemical and biological weapons if Iraq was invaded by land, but that use prior to this – even during aerial bombardment of Iraq – was unlikely.*

144. Despite an extensive search, no evidence has come to light which would indicate that this point had been conveyed to the public by any government minister in the period before the invasion of Iraq. No statements by the Prime Minister refer to the low probability of Iraq using chemical and biological weapons externally other than during an invasion of Iraq. In fact, the Prime Minister repeatedly indicated that Iraq's illicit weapons were a worldwide threat (see section 1.2 above), which would have indicated to his audience that the external and unprovoked use of chemical and biological weapons was in fact likely.

145. Moreover, drafted statements to convey the point that Iraq would only be likely to use chemical and biological weapons during an invasion were removed from final documents.

146. In response to the text in the 19 September 2002 draft of the September dossier quoted above, the Downing Street chief of staff, Jonathan Powell, wrote an email on that same day to Alastair Campbell (then the Prime Minister's director of communications), John Scarlett (chair of the JIC) and David Manning (the Prime Minister's foreign affairs and defence adviser). In this email, he advised a change to the dossier:[77]

'I think the statement on p19 that 'Saddam is prepared to use chemical and biological weapons if he believes his regime is under threat' is a bit of a problem. It backs up the Don McIntyre argument that there is no CBW threat and we will only create one if we attack him. I think you should redraft the para.'

147. The text of the dossier was duly modified, and the published version stated simply:

'intelligence indicates that as part of Iraq's military planning Saddam is willing to use chemical and biological weapons'

148. The 'problem' identified by Powell was not that the dossier misrepresented intelligence assessments, which it did not – it simply restated the judgements of the March 2002 interdepartmental paper and the 9 September 2002 JIC assessment. In the absence of any other explanation, it is reasonable to conclude that the accurate publication of the intelligence assessment was deemed politically inconvenient. As a result a text was circulated that would have led its audience to believe that Iraq was willing to use chemical and biological weapons *in general*, rather than in the very specific circumstance referred to in the intelligence assessments.

149. Mr Powell remains in his position as Downing Street chief of staff, and there is no public record of a reprimand from the Prime Minister to Mr Powell for encouraging government officials to mislead the public. As a result, Mr Powell's actions have received the *de facto* endorsement of his superior, the Prime Minister.

150. Similarly, the first two drafts of the Prime Minister's foreword included a statement that accurately represented the intelligence assessment:[78]

'The case I make is not that Saddam could launch a nuclear attack on London or another part of the UK (He could not).'

151. The Prime Minister read a draft of this foreword and recommended changes to it.[79] In the very next draft of the foreword, later on 17 September 2002, this statement was taken out of the text of the foreword.[80] As a result, it would be reasonable to infer that the omission of the above text, and hence from the published version, of the foreword was directed by or consented to by the Prime Minister.

152. The removal from published material of text that would contradict those who envisioned that Iraq could use NBC weapons against the UK – the view represented by the London Evening Standard headline on 24 September 2002 that the UK was '45 minutes from attack' – strongly indicates that the Prime Minister was ready to allow a highly alarmist view of Iraq's weapons to spread. This view was in direct contrast with the perspective of the intelligence services, but enabled a political climate of fear to be generated in which an invasion of Iraq could be justified to a substantial proportion of the population.

153. The Prime Minister has insisted subsequently that he did not know that the claim from the September dossier that Iraq could use chemical and biological weapons in 45 minutes referred to short-range battlefield weapons, rather than longer range missiles that could threaten other countries. If true, this would reveal a high level of negligence, in which the Prime Minister allowed himself to be unaware of the potential dangers that he was exposing the Middle Eastern

region to in confronting Iraq with the threat of force. However, even if he did not know to what form of weapons this particular allegation referred to, he had at his disposal a number of JIC assessments that envisioned that Saddam Hussein would only use chemical or biological weapons outside Iraq's territory *if* Iraq itself were attacked. *That he did not reveal this crucial information indicates strongly that he was allowing a highly misleading impression of Iraq's potential threat to become widespread.*

2.5 Non-evaluation of the Iraqi declaration made in December 2002

154. Security Council Resolution 1441, paragraph 3, stated that 'the Government of Iraq shall provide to UNMOVIC, the IAEA, and the Council, not later than 30 days from the date of this resolution, a currently accurate, full, and complete declaration of all aspects of its programmes to develop' NBC weapons. Iraq submitted this declaration on the evening of 7-8 December 2002. Shortly after submission of the document, members of the UK government began to denounce it. The Prime Minister told the House of Commons on 25 February 2003:[81]

'On 8 December he submitted the declaration denying he had any WMD, a statement not a single member of the international community seriously believes.'

155. On 18 March 2003, the Prime Minister declared categorically:[82]

'the 8 December declaration is false'

156. The claim by the Prime Minister that 'not a single member of the international community seriously believes' Iraq's denial was knowingly false: President Putin of Russia had been standing alongside Mr Blair at a London press conference when he declared:[83]

'Russia does not have in its possession any trustworthy data which would support the existence of nuclear weapons or any weapons of mass destruction in Iraq, and we have not received from our partners such information'.

157. More seriously, the Butler report (§363) recorded:

'We also noted the limited time given to evaluation of the Iraqi declaration of 7 December. Considerable effort was made by DIS staff immediately on its receipt to sift and analyse its contents. Their initial findings were reported by the Assessments Staff on 13 December. Further DIS work on the declaration was captured in a JIC paper on 18 December, properly described as *'An Initial Assessment of Iraq's WMD Declaration'*. Thereafter, despite its importance to the determination of whether Iraq was in further material breach of its disarmament obligations under United Nations Security Council Resolution 1441, the JIC made no further assessment.'

158. Therefore, the Prime Minister's allegations about the Iraqi declaration on, *inter alia*, 25 February and 18 March 2003, were based upon an initial assessment conducted by the Defence Intelligence Staff (DIS), rather than a full assessment. Given that the declaration was 12,000 pages long, it is difficult to

imagine how a concerted evaluation could have been made by the DIS in the period of less than ten days following its submission. In addition, this episode demonstrates the lack of an attempt by the government, led by the Prime Minister, to fully evaluate the information it received.

159. The declaration acquires significance because the UN inspectors found parts of it to be useful. Hans Blix told the Security Council on 19 December 2002:[84]

'Although it must be noted that much of what Iraq has provided in the weapons part of its Declaration is not new, there are some sections of new material. In the chemical weapons field, Iraq has further explained its account of the material balance of precursors for chemical warfare agents. Although it does not resolve outstanding issues on this subject, it may help to achieve a better understanding of the fate of the precursors. In the missile area, there is a good deal of information regarding Iraq's activities in the past few years.'

160. Dr Blix elaborated on 27 January 2003:[85]

'In the fields of missiles and biotechnology, the declaration contains a good deal of new material and information covering the period from 1998 and onward. This is welcome.'

161. *It seems that the UK did not have intelligence material with which to disagree with Dr Blix's statement on the usefulness of the declaration. However, they continued to portray it as inadequate, and used this as part of the justification for war.*

2.6 Not telling the public and Parliament about other threats

162. A consistent approach of the Prime Minister in the period from the start of 2002 has been to link the issues of Iraq's alleged NBC weapons and international terrorism. Some of the most notable examples of this linkage are as follows.

163. The Prime Minister told a press conference on 13 January 2003:[86]

'Now I simply say to you, it is a matter of time unless we act and take a stand before terrorism and weapons of mass destruction come together, and I regard them as two sides of the same coin. And the reason why Iraq is important is Iraq is the issue around which this has come to have focus.'

164. The Prime Minister said to the House of Commons on 3 February 2003:[87]

'Over the past few weeks, we have seen powerful evidence of the continuing terrorist threat [. . .] At the same time, we know too that Iraq is not alone in developing WMD [. . .] I repeat my warning: unless we take a decisive stand now, as an international community, it is only a matter of time before these threats come together.'

165. The Prime Minister said to the House of Commons on 18 March 2003:[88]

'Those two threats [terrorism and states with NBC weapons] have, of course, different motives and different origins, but they share one basic common view: they detest the freedom, democracy and tolerance that are the hallmarks of our way of life. At the moment, I accept fully that the association between the two is loose – but it is hardening. The possibility of the two coming together – of terrorist groups in possession of weapons of mass destruction or even of a so-called dirty radiological bomb – is now, in my judgment, a real and present danger to Britain and its national security.'

166. The Prime Minister said in a speech on 5 March 2004:[89]

'I asked for more intelligence on the issue not just of terrorism but also of WMD. [. . .] But then we had to confront the states with WMD. We had to take a stand. We had to force conformity with international obligations that for years had been breached with the world turning a blind eye. For 12 years Saddam had defied calls to disarm. [. . .] my judgement then and now is that the risk of this new global terrorism and its interaction with states or organisations or individuals proliferating WMD, is one I simply am not prepared to run.'

167. Despite the many speeches by the Prime Minister on this theme, not once did he mention the actual assessment of the intelligence services – referred to in the last speech quoted above – of the likely consequences of an invasion of Iraq on the threat to the UK from terrorism. The Prime Minister has increasingly justified the war on Iraq upon the argument that it would lessen the risk of a terrorist attack; he did not mention that the intelligence services were giving precisely the opposite assessment:[90]

'The JIC assessed that al-Qaida and associated groups continued to represent by far the greatest terrorist threat to Western interests, and *that threat would be heightened by military action against Iraq.*

The JIC assessed that any collapse of the Iraqi regime *would increase the risk of chemical and biological warfare technology or agents finding their way into the hands of terrorists*, not necessarily al-Qaida.'

168. The response of the British government to the report from the Intelligence and Security Committee, which reported the JIC assessment, acknowledged:[91]

'The Committee notes (paragraphs 127 and 128) that the JIC assessed that any collapse of the Iraqi regime would increase the risk of chemical and biological warfare technology or agents finding their way into the hands of terrorists, *and that the Prime Minister was aware of this.*'

169. In addition, JIC assessments reported that Iraq's NBC capabilities were judged to be lesser in scale, and less of a direct challenge to UK interests, than those of other states of concern.[92] None of this information was disclosed to the public by the government, despite it being highly germane to the assessment of whether the Prime Minister was correct in making the argument that the war on Iraq would abate the threat from terrorism.

3. Failure to withdraw material found to be false, or which should have been found to be false

3.1 Evaluating past intelligence after the re-introduction of inspectors

170. The Butler report (§362) recorded its surprise at how the British intelligence services were not asked for a re-evaluation of intelligence on Iraqi weapons after the introduction of UN weapons inspectors in November 2002:

> 'we are surprised that neither policy-makers nor the intelligence community, as the generally negative results of UNMOVIC inspections became increasingly apparent, conducted a formal re-evaluation of the quality of the intelligence and hence of the assessments made on it.'

171. This is remarkable, given that the inspectors were visiting the sites that the British government had previously named as sites of concern. William Ehrman, the then Director General of Defence/Intelligence at the Foreign and Commonwealth Office (and now the chairman of the JIC), told the Foreign Affairs Committee on 27 June 2003 that 'Every single site in the dossier has been visited by UNMOVIC' prior to the launching of the invasion.[93]

172. The examination of the sites named in the September dossier had resulted in no traces of nuclear, chemical or biological weapons programmes.

173. The only site mentioned in the dossier in relation to illicit nuclear activities was al-Sharqat complex in north western Iraq. The dossier alleged that 'part of the site has been rebuilt', and was producing nitric acid, which could be used for the purification of uranium. UNMOVIC and/or IAEA inspection teams visited this site on 2 and 9 January 2003. Dr Mohamed El Baradei, the director general of the International Atomic Energy Agency (IAEA), told the Security Council on 7 March 2003:[94]

> 'There is *no indication of resumed nuclear activities* in those buildings that were identified through the use of satellite imagery as being reconstructed or newly erected since 1998, nor any indication of nuclear-related prohibited activities at any inspected sites.'

174. The first site mentioned in the dossier in relation to an illicit chemical weapons programme was the Fallujah II plant, 100 km north-west of Baghdad: the dossier alleged that this plant was engaged in the production of chlorine. By contrast, UNMOVIC visited the site at least five times between 9 December 2002 and 2 March 2003 and recorded:[95]

> 'The chlorine plant is currently inoperative.'

175. No findings of any significance were reported at the other sites (Ibn Sina Company and al-Qa'Qa') mentioned as being of relevance to Iraq's chemical weapons programme in the September dossier.

176. The first site alleged in the September dossier to be of relevance to Iraq's biological weapons programme was al-Dawra Foot and Mouth Disease Vaccine Institute. This was a report from a journalist accompanying inspectors:[96]

'By the time the inspectors left the plant today, after four hours, they had concluded that the plant was no longer operational – not for the production of toxins, and not for animal vaccines either. Reporters who were allowed to wander through the plant after the inspectors left found the place largely in ruins. Apparently, it had been *abandoned by the Iraqis after 1996*, when the weapons inspectors took heavy cutting equipment to the fermenters, containers and pressurized tubing and valves used in the toxin production.'

177. The second such site mentioned in the September dossier was the Castor Oil Production Plant at Fallujah. UNMOVIC inspectors recorded:[97]

'The castor oil extraction plant at Fallujah III was destroyed in December 1998. UNMOVIC inspections since December 2002 have verified that the bombed castor oil extraction plant at Fallujah III has been reconstructed on a larger scale. However, the *production seems to have ceased in July 2001.*'

178. The work of inspectors thus indicated that there was no indication that the sites mentioned in the September dossier were engaged in the illicit production of material for NBC programmes. In at least three cases, the plants mentioned in the September dossier do not appear to have even been operational at the time the dossier was written.

179. Furthermore, UNMOVIC reported on how it was unlikely that they were being misled into making invalid conclusions by Iraqi deception activities. Hans Blix told the Security Council on 14 February 2003:[98]

'Since we arrived in Iraq, we have conducted more than 400 inspections covering more than 300 sites. All inspections were performed without notice, and access was almost always provided promptly. In no case have we seen convincing evidence that the Iraqi side knew in advance that the inspectors were coming. [. . .] we note that access to sites has so far been without problems, including those that had never been declared or inspected, as well as to Presidential sites and private residences.'

180. Hans Blix went on to tell the Security Council on 7 March 2003 that 'the numerous initiatives, which are now taken by the Iraqi side with a view to resolving some long-standing open disarmament issues, can be seen as "active", or even "proactive"'.[99]

181. With these findings, therefore, it would have been clear that the intelligence upon which the September dossier was based was insufficient, and quite probably wrong. However, not only did the Prime Minister fail to order a review of that intelligence, but he also reaffirmed its validity, despite contrary information from the inspectors. The British government's failure to re-evaluate its claims, despite this 'proactive' cooperation from Iraq, demonstrates that there was no attempt to ascertain the likely state of Iraq's weapons prior to the invasion. On the 19 March 2003, just before the invasion began, the Prime Minister replied to a written parliamentary question on this issue:[100]

Paul Flynn: To ask the Prime Minister what plans he has to publish amendments to his assessment in the document 'Iraq's Weapons of Mass Destruction' presented to the

House in September 2002 arising from the evidence of UNMOVIC inspectors on Iraqi (a) bases, (b) presidential palaces and (c) uranium imports.

The Prime Minister: I have no plans to publish an amended version of the dossier presented in September 2002, the contents of which *still accurately reflect our assessment* of the position with regard to Iraq's proscribed weapons programmes.

182. *The Prime Minister was thus reaffirming the validity of crucial allegations that he had made previously, without re-examining them in light of the large amount of new and detailed information available to him that cast severe doubt upon those allegations.*

3.2 Discredited sources

183. The Butler report recorded that at least four sets of intelligence reports that were of considerable significance to the government in making its case about Iraq were subsequently either withdrawn or had serious doubt cast upon them. Three of these were from sources on Iraq's alleged weapons, whilst one was from a source of information on Iraq's alleged deception and concealment activities.

184. The first of these, recorded in the Butler report at §405, consists of two reports from a 'new source on trial': the first of these 'did provide significant assurance to those drafting the Government's dossier that active, current production of chemical and biological agent was taking place'. However, both reports were withdrawn by MI6 in July 2003, as 'the sourcing chain had by then been *discredited*'.

185. The second of these was from a subsource who reported 'on Iraqi chemical and biological programmes and intentions', and had links to opposition groups. The Butler report recorded (§403): 'We have been told that post-war validation by SIS has *raised serious doubts* about the reliability of reporting from this new sub-source'. This is presumably the individual who provided the information that Iraq could use chemical and biological weapons within 45 minutes (see §512 of the Butler report).

186. The third of these was the second major source for intelligence reports on Iraqi deception and concealment activities. The Butler report recorded (at p.89, note 13):

'We have, however, been told that post-war validation by SIS of its sources has led to *doubts about the reliability of the reports* provided by the source who provided the smaller proportion of the reporting.'

187. The fourth of these was the source for the 'vast majority of the intelligence' on Iraq's mobile biological facilities. Based upon a briefing by the head of MI6 in May 2004, the Butler report stated (§409):

'for the purposes of our Review, we conclude that there must be some *doubts about the reliability of all the reports received from this source* via the liaison service. We also conclude that intelligence reports received in 2000 which suggested that Iraq had recently-produced biological agent were seriously flawed.'

188. As these four sources were all under doubt from at least July 2003 (in the case of the first source listed above), key allegations about Iraq's illicit programmes also lost credibility. However, this was not made public until the Butler report was released in July 2004, even though, had it been released, it would have allowed a more honest public assessment of the case that had been made for war.

189. In fact, the Prime Minister continued to affirm the validity of the intelligence that he had been drawing upon prior to the war itself, *at the same time as the intelligence services were retracting or doubting that intelligence*.

190. On 2 June 2003, the Prime Minister said:[101]

'I stand absolutely 100% behind the evidence, based on intelligence, that we presented to people [. . .] I have no doubt at all, as I said to you earlier, that the assessments that were made by the British intelligence services will turn out to be correct.'

191. On 8 July 2003, the Prime Minister reaffirmed this at length to the House of Commons Liaison Committee:[102]

'You know, you asked me right at the very outset, do I stand by the essential case? I do stand by the essential case. *I also stand entirely by the intelligence we put in the September dossier*, which after all was the main thing that we brought before Parliament [. . .]. I simply want to tell you today and, through you, the country that I believe we did the right thing, I stand 100% by it, and I think that our intelligence services gave us the correct intelligence and information at the time. [. . .] I do not believe that our intelligence will be shown to be wrong at all. I think it will be shown to be right. I have absolutely no doubt whatever that he was trying to reconstitute weapons of mass destruction programmes and *that the intelligence that we were getting out of Iraq about those programmes and about the attempt to conceal them was correct*. [. . .] that intelligence *I have no doubt at all was valid intelligence*.'

192. On 30 July 2003, the Prime Minister said at his monthly press conference:

'I believe the intelligence we received is correct. So that is my view, it has been my view all the way through [. . .]'

193. On 25 January 2004, at least six months after MI6 had withdrawn key reports on Iraq's weapons, the Prime Minister was still defending the validity of the intelligence he had presented, in an interview with *The Observer*:[103]

'It is absurd to say in respect of any intelligence that it is infallible, but if you ask me what I believe, *I believe the intelligence was correct*, and I think in the end we will have an explanation.'

194. The Prime Minister has asserted that he was not aware of the withdrawal of the reports on the 'new source on trial' until the Butler process was complete in July 2004. The Prime Minister has thus acknowledged that he was in a position of serious ignorance for at least 12 months, during which time he continued to assert the validity of information derived from discredited sources.

As the Prime Minister was continuing to make frequent remarks on the validity of pre-war intelligence, for him not to review that intelligence, and make himself aware that four major sources that he had previously cited had now come under serious doubt, indicates grave negligence.

3.3 Interfering with reporting from US-led inspection process to prevent past statements being discredited

195. The Prime Minister only changed his allegations on Iraq's weapons at the end of January 2004, when the former head of the US-led Iraq Survey Group (ISG) David Kay told the US Senate Armed Services Committee on 28 January:[104]

'we were almost all wrong [. . .] it is highly unlikely that there were large stockpiles of deployed militarised chemical and biological weapons there.'

196. The negative reports on Iraq's past weapons production and retention undoubtedly caused considerable political embarrassment to the Prime Minister. His testimony to the House of Commons Liaison Committee on 3 February 2004 was very different to the account he provided in his interview with the Observer less than ten days before, quoted above. Now he defended intelligence procedures, but not the substance of the intelligence reports:[105]

'I have to take account of what David Kay has said in the last few days. He was the Head of the Iraq Survey Group and I said all the way through, "Let us wait for this Survey Group". It is not a question, as it were, of changing our position; it is a question of recognising the fact that though there has been ample evidence of weapons of mass destruction programmes and capability, the actual weapons have not been found as yet in Iraq and the view of the Head of the Iraq Survey Group is that he does not believe that the intelligence in relation to the stockpiles of weapons was correct. Now, that is exactly what we need to look into.'

197. However, rather than admitting the flaws of pre-war intelligence, there is strong evidence that one tactic has been to attempt to modify the substance of the reports of the Iraq Survey Group (ISG), in order to make them less politically damaging to the British government.

198. On 8 March 2004, John Scarlett – the then chair of the Joint Intelligence Committee, who took over as head of MI6 on 1 August 2004 – wrote an email to the new head of the ISG, Charles Duelfer. This was immediately prior to Mr Duelfer making a scheduled status report to Congress. According to *The Times*, Mr Scarlett:[106]

'suggested that the ISG report should be cut from 200 pages of detailed analysis to 20, and left sufficiently vague to protect Mr Blair's stand on Iraq's weapons menace. He wanted the report to keep alive the prospect that deadly weapons could still be found. In a confidential e-mail sent to the ISG team in Baghdad, Mr Scarlett is alleged to have asked them to add ten golden nuggets to their report which prolonged the idea that there were weapons of mass destruction. One of these alleged nuggets was that Iraq was developing smallpox weapons. He also wanted mention that Iraq had mobile biological weapons laboratories and sophisticated equipment for use in nuclear weapons research.'

199. The receipt of this email was acknowledged by Mr Duelfer in an interview with *The Guardian*, who confirmed that Mr Scarlett suggested that he include items in his report.[107]

200. If a full inquiry and the appropriate reprimands are not forthcoming from the government into these allegations, it would demonstrate that the Prime Minister has endorsed the actions by Mr Scarlett, to distort the ISG's findings in order for them to be more palatable politically. **If the allegations are true, it provides further decisive indications that the attempt by the British government to mislead the public and Members of Parliament on the subject of Iraq's weapons did not end with the invasion, but has continued to the present day.**

4. Making a secret agreement with President Bush to remove Saddam Hussein by force if necessary

201. The evidence available to the public strongly indicates that the Prime Minister understood that the United States was planning to invade Iraq from late 2001, unless Saddam Hussein was deposed through other means; that he made a decision to support the United States in this action during the course of mid-2002; and that he used the claims about Iraq's weapons and about non-cooperation with the UN weapons inspectors throughout this period as a way to win support from the public and other countries. In effect, the Prime Minister had committed the UK to assist the US with the invasion of Iraq, but had not disclosed this commitment to Parliament, to his own Cabinet or to the British public. It may be that there is evidence that has not yet been disclosed which would call this interpretation into question. However, the failure of the Prime Minister to provide informative denials to the statements of senior and respected officials indicates that the accounts of these individuals are true.

202. According to Sir Christopher Meyer, the former British ambassador to the United States, the Prime Minister was aware that the US would invade Iraq during the term of the first Bush administration from 20 September 2001. The Prime Minister and President Bush had dinner on that date at the White House, which Meyer also attended. Meyer's account was contained in an article in *Vanity Fair*:[108]

'On Thursday, September 20, Tony Blair arrived in Washington for a meeting at the White House. Until now, many assumed his and Bush's early talks had been limited to the coming war in Afghanistan. In fact, they also spoke of Iraq. At a dinner in the White House, attended also by Colin Powell, Condi Rice, and the British ambassador to the United States, Sir Christopher Meyer, Bush made clear that he was determined to topple Saddam. "Rumors were already flying that Bush would use 9/11 as a pretext to attack Iraq," Meyer remembers. "On the one hand, Blair came with a very strong message-don't get distracted; the priorities were al-Qaeda, Afghanistan, the Taliban. Bush said, 'I agree with you, Tony. We must deal with this first. But when we have dealt with Afghanistan, *we must come back to Iraq*.'"'

203. On 29 January 2002, President Bush declared in his State of the Union address that Iraq was part of an 'axis of evil'. This was followed up by explicit commitments in public to effect a change in the Iraqi leadership. On 4 April 2002, he told British journalist Trevor Macdonald:[109]

'I made up my mind that Saddam needs to go. That's about all I'm willing to share with you. [. . .] I'm confident that we can lead a coalition to pressure Saddam Hussein and to deal with Saddam Hussein.'

204. This was followed up by President Bush's statement at a press conference with Tony Blair in Crawford, Texas on 6 April 2002. He said:[110]

'I explained to the Prime Minister that the policy of my government is the removal of Saddam and that all options are on the table.'

205. Thus it was clear to the Prime Minister that the United States government was intent on bringing about a change in the Iraqi leadership. Thus if internal coup attempts failed, and if Saddam Hussein could not be coerced into leaving the country, the Prime Minister could expect that an invasion of Iraq by US forces would follow.

206. The evidence strongly indicates that the response of the British government to these developments was to give its support to the objectives of the Bush administration. Firstly, the Prime Minister gave his clear verbal support to the approach of President Bush. On 7 April 2002, the day after President Bush had said that his government's policy was to remove Saddam Hussein, Mr Blair said in a prepared speech at the George Bush Senior Presidential Library:[111]

'when America is fighting for those values, then, however tough, we fight with her. No grandstanding, no offering implausible but impractical advice from the comfort of the touchline, no wishing away the hard not the easy choices on terrorism and WMD, or making peace in the Middle East, but working together, side by side. [. . .] If the world makes the right choices now – at this time of destiny – we will get there. And *Britain will be at America's side in doing it*.'

207. Secondly, in the months immediately after this statement, British military personnel commenced meetings with US personnel to plan an invasion of Iraq. Air Marshal Brian Burridge, the national contingent commander for Operation Telic (the invasion of Iraq), told the House of Commons Defence Select Committee on 11 June 2003 that this planning began in 'early in June or July' of 2002.[112] He also described the reason for the planning process:[113]

'We began looking at Iraq planning in the summer. We had no timetable, but it was put to me that if the UK was at any stage likely to participate, then best we at least understand the planning and influence the planning for the better. At no stage did we say "Here is the end date by which we are going to do this". What we did have was a couple of windows. We said ideally it makes sense either to do this in the spring of 2003 or autumn of 2003.'

208. Whilst contingency planning is not to be confused with the political decision to invade, it is clear that at this stage the British government was choosing to participate in a planning process that it knew the US administration had already committed itself to implementing, if other methods of removing Saddam Hussein did not succeed.

209. Thirdly, the changed policy towards Iraq was reflected in interdepartmental advice given to ministers in March 2002. The first in the list of the 'current objectives towards Iraq' was:[114]

'the reintegration of a law-abiding Iraq, which does not possess WMD or threaten its neighbours, into the international community. Implicitly, this cannot occur with Saddam in power'

210. Thus from March 2002, the British government recognised that its objective should be removal of Saddam Hussein from power. As interdepartmental advice from March 2002 recognised, this would likely require military force:[115]

'In sum, despite the considerable difficulties, *the use of overriding force in a ground campaign* is the only option that we can be confident will remove Saddam and bring Iraq back into the international community.'

211. However, this advice from March 2002 also recognised that 'offensive military action against Iraq could only be justified if Iraq were held to be in breach of United Nations Security Council Resolution 687'. Therefore, the five permanent members of the UN Security Council, and at least nine of all its members, would need to concur that Iraq had committed such a breach. This could only be achieved under three possible conditions:[116]

'They would need to be convinced that Iraq was in breach of its obligations regarding WMD, and ballistic missiles. Such proof would need to be incontrovertible and of large-scale activity. *Current intelligence is insufficiently robust to meet this criterion* . . .
or
If P5 unity could be obtained, Iraq refused to readmit UN inspectors after a clear ultimatum by the UN Security Council.
or
The UN inspectors were re-admitted to Iraq and found sufficient evidence of WMD activity or were again expelled trying to do so.'

212. Therefore, the only way in which the British government recognised that it could justify an invasion of Iraq would be to use the United Nations weapons inspectors to provide a pretext for an invasion. The evidence indicates that the Prime Minister recognised that the work of UNMOVIC to verify Iraq's disarmament would not be allowed to substitute for an invasion.

213. In July 2002, the Prime Minister had a 15-minute conversation with President Bush; a senior US official from the Vice-President's office who read a transcript of this conversation gave *Vanity Fair* a description of its contents:[117]

'The way it read was that, come what may, Saddam was going to go; they said they were going forward, *they were going to take out the regime*, and they were doing the right thing. Blair did not need any convincing. There was no, 'Come on, Tony, we've got to get you on board'. I remember reading it and then thinking, OK, now I know what we're going to be doing for the next year. [. . .] *it was a done deal.*'

214. The Butler report gives the strong indication that the British government accepted that this 'done deal' was for the UK to engage with presentational activity and give its military support, in return for which President Bush would enable the Prime Minister to use the weapons inspectors as a pretext.

215. The Butler report recorded that at the 6 April 2002 Crawford meeting, Mr Blair and President Bush discussed 'the need for effective presentational activity',[118] namely:[119]

'The importance of presentational activity on Iraq's breaches (and other issues) to persuade other members of the United Nations Security Council as well as domestic audiences of the case for action to enforce disarmament.'

216. That the reintroduction of weapons inspectors could serve as a pretext for military action was a consistent theme of US-UK planning over the next months:[120]

'The role of the United Nations – in building an international consensus on the need for action to tackle Iraq's prohibited weapons programmes; in the re-engagement of inspectors to investigate the extent and scale of those programmes; and *ultimately in providing legitimacy for any military action to enforce disarmament* – was discussed further at a meeting between the Foreign Secretary and Secretary of State Powell at a meeting at the Hamptons, New York, on 20 August 2002,and between the Prime Minister and the President at Camp David on 7 September 2002. It is clear from the departmental papers we have seen that the UK championed the role of the United Nations at that meeting.'

217. The nature of the 7 September 2002 meeting between the Prime Minister and President Bush was explained in more detail in Bob Woodward's book, *Plan of Attack*, which was written with the compliance of the White House:[121]

On the morning of Sept. 7, 2002, Blair left London on a transatlantic flight to see Bush at Camp David. In Blair's conversations with Bush, *it was increasingly clear to the prime minister how committed Bush was to action*. [. . .]

Bush looked Blair in the eye. 'Saddam Hussein is a threat. And we must work together to deal with this threat, and the world will be better off without him.' Bush recalled that he was 'probing' and 'pushing' the Prime Minister. He said it might require – would probably entail – war. Blair might have to send British troops. *'I'm with you,' the Prime Minister replied, looking Bush back in the eye, pledging flat out to commit British military force if necessary,* the critical promise Bush had been seeking.

218. There is no indication that this pledge by the Prime Minister to commit British military forces was conditional upon non-compliance with UN weapons

inspectors. The US President had committed his administration to removing Saddam Hussein, come what may. This might not require an invasion to achieve, although President Bush recognised it probably would. Thus the Prime Minister was committing British forces to an invasion, except in the unlikely event that Saddam Hussein would be ousted by other means before that invasion took place.

219. These commitments given by the Prime Minister to the US President were not revealed to his cabinet, to Parliament or to the public. In fact, the Prime Minister repeatedly said that no decisions had yet been taken. The Prime Minister's assurances to a member of his Cabinet were recorded in the diary of former International Development Secretary Clare Short:[122]

> 'On 26 July [2002], she wrote, she raised her "simmering worry about Iraq" in a meeting with Blair. She wanted a debate on Iraq in the next Cabinet meeting, but he said it was unnecessary because "it would get hyped . . . He said nothing decided and wouldn't be over summer."[. . .]
>
> As late as 9 September, Short's diary records, "T[ony] B[lair] gave me assurances when I asked for Iraq to be discussed at Cabinet that no decision made and not imminent."'

220. To the public and Parliament, the Prime Minister continued to emphasise that he had not committed himself to changing the Iraqi leadership. On 25 February 2003, he told the House of Commons:[123]

> 'I detest his regime. But even now he can save it by complying with the UN's demand. Even now, we are prepared to go the extra step to achieve disarmament peacefully.'

221. If any of the accounts quoted above from Bob Woodward, *Vanity Fair* or the Butler report are accurate, it was not true that no decision had been taken by the Prime Minister. In fact, these accounts strongly indicate that by 9 September 2002, Mr Blair had agreed to commit British forces in support of US troops if they were to invade Iraq. The Prime Minister has not provided any information to discredit these accounts. Therefore, it is reasonable to conclude that the Prime Minister had made a secret alliance to go to war by 9 September 2002, and that his subsequent presentation of material on Iraq's NBC weapons were an attempt to win public and international support for a predetermined policy outcome.

Chapter II

Impeachment

222. The second chapter will discuss the context in which the charge of impeachment is being introduced and looks at the law and procedure of impeachment today. There is no doubt that although previous Select Committees have recommended that the right to impeach be formally abandoned, this has not happened. In 1967 the Select Committee on Parliamentary Privilege noted that legislation would be required to give effect to this recommendation. No such legislation has been introduced. In 1998-99 the Joint Committee on Parliamentary Privilege Report noted that the procedure 'may be considered obsolete' but that de facto obsolescence does not remove the need for legislation (section 2).

223. The report shows that the historic grounds for impeachment cover the charges against the Prime Minister, and as such will focus on; subversion of the constitution (the usurpation of power), the abuse of power and the betrayal of trust (section 3 and 5). In conclusion, the report will consider the use of impeachment as a last resort to hold the Prime Minister to account (section 4) and will detail the impeachable offences of the Prime Minister (section 5).

1. Summary

224. In 1999 the Parliamentary Joint Committee on Parliamentary Privilege[124], explained *'Under this [...] procedure, all persons, whether peers or commoners, may be prosecuted and tried by the two Houses for any crimes whatsoever.'* As is explained below, there is a clearly established procedure for impeachment in Britain. Impeachment is a parliamentary word for an accusation and arising from this there can be an impeachment trial. However the phrase, 'x was impeached' can be used to mean either that he was accused, or tried or convicted. Thus Warren Hastings, back in the eighteenth century was accused and tried but not convicted.

225. It only takes one MP to make the

accusation of High Crimes and Misdemeanours against a public official for the impeachment process to begin. Once the accuser has presented his or her proofs to the Commons and if the House agrees that there is a case to answer, a committee is established to draw up articles of impeachment. The Lords are notified and if they agree to the articles they then appoint prosecutors to try the case before the Lords who are the judges. If there is a conviction the Commons decides the sentence.

226. In law, any individual can be tried for any offence. According to precedents discussed below, impeachments were mainly used to try government officials. The charges fall into two categories Treason, and High Crimes and Misdemeanours. Offences such as corruption or dishonesty were sometimes used to bring a charge of Treason and sometimes of High Crimes and Misdemeanours. The most modern discussions of what can be considered impeachable offences according to the precedents in Parliament have been in the USA, whose own impeachment law is based on UK practice. Some US lawyers argue that private conduct by the President is not impeachable according to UK precedents; there is a broader agreement that Presidential misconduct which damages the government is impeachable.

227. An examination of legal history and of the original charges used in impeachment trials since the fourteenth century indicates that official misconduct including dishonesty and negligence that damages the government and the country is impeachable. *Damage to the constitution* and the *supremacy of Parliament and the rule of law* have all been considered impeachable in England and Wales. At various periods impeachment has been used with respect to issues purely of policy and though it is hard to draw clear lines between policy and issues of competence and truthfulness, the former are *less* impeachable today and the latter *more* impeachable. Ultimately, the law in England and Wales is written that an offence is impeachable if the House of Commons declares it to be the case.

228. *This report argues that the Prime Minister's refusal to resign for his misleading statements meant that he breached parliamentary conventions. Therefore, not only should he face impeachment for misleading Parliament, but judgments should also be cast for his failure to respect constitutional conventions by resigning. In addition to these charges, there is evidence that prior to March 2003, he made an agreement with President Bush to overthrow Saddam Hussein. As in the case against Palmerston in 1848 (see below), this charge is equally impeachable.*

229. Parliament itself as well as authorities such as Erskine May (see Annex A) and William Holdsworth have placed impeachment as the foundation of the modern constitutional conventions upon which we rely. Perhaps the most important of the conventions or laws of the constitution is that ministers must not mislead Parliament. Under this government the convention has been applied twice; to Beverley Hughes and Peter Mandelson, requiring them to resign their offices. This report concludes that the Prime Minister misled Parliament and the country to a vastly greater extent than either of these ministers and yet he remains

in office, refusing any further examination of his conduct. Any MP who tries, as John Baron did, to discuss the Prime Minister's misconduct in the House of Commons is called to order by the Speaker of the House. The only way to discuss misconduct and misleading statements in Parliament is through impeachment.

230. According to authorities of the constitution, impeachment is meant to be the means of last resort. As Walter Bagehot put it, writing from the Poplars, Wimbledon in 1872: *'there are two checks [on government] – one ancient and coarse, the other modern and delicate. The first is the check of impeachment.'* The modern and delicate conventions of our unwritten constitution have collapsed, only the ancient use of Parliament as a court of law is left to us.

2. The law and procedure of impeachment today

231. As recently as September 2003, the House of Commons library produced a note on impeachment[125] which states: 'The ancient procedure of impeachment is described in the report of the Joint Committee on Parliamentary Privilege'. This Committee, which reported in 1999, described the process as follows:[126]

'Under this [. . .] procedure, all persons, whether peers or commoners, may be prosecuted and tried by the two Houses for any crimes whatsoever. The House of Commons determines when an impeachment should be instituted. A member, in his place, first charges the accused of high treason, or of certain crimes and misdemeanours. After supporting his charge with proofs the member moves for impeachment. If the accusation is found on examination by the House to have sufficient grounds to justify further proceedings, the motion is put to the House. If agreed, a member (or members) are ordered by the House to go to the bar of the House of Lords. There in the name of the House of Commons and of all the Commons of the United Kingdom, the member impeaches the accused person. A Commons committee is then appointed to draw up articles of impeachment which are debated. When agreed they are ingrossed and delivered to the Lords. The Lords obtain written answers from the accused which are communicated to the Commons. The Commons may then communicate a reply to the Lords. If the accused is a peer, he is attached by order to that House. If a commoner, he is arrested and delivered to Black Rod. The Lords may release the accused on bail. The Commons appoints 'managers' for the trial to prepare attendance of witnesses on his behalf, and is entitled to defence by counsel. When the case, including examination and re-examination, is concluded, the Lord High Steward puts to each peer, (beginning with the junior baron) the question on the first of the charges: then to each peer the question on the second charge and so on. If found guilty, judgement is not pronounced unless and until demanded by the Commons (which may, at this stage, pardon the accused). An impeachment may continue from session to session, or over a dissolution. Under the Act of Settlement the sovereign has no right of pardon. The last impeachment was in 1805 (Lord Melville). The procedure has not been widely adopted in the Commonwealth. However, it survives, in a somewhat different form, in the constitution of the United States of America.'

232. Standard texts on constitutional law and the history of English law consistently agree, with regards to impeachment, that while it is outmoded, it is

not defunct. According to *Holdsworth's History of English Law*, which remains a standard textbook in Universities and was first published in 1903:[127]

> '...it is improbable that this procedure will ever be revived...On the other hand it is still legally possible, so that, whatever may be the political probabilities, it is impossible to treat it as wholly obsolete.'

3. Impeachable offences in their historical context

3.1 Most recent cases

233. There have been more than seventy cases of impeachment in English history. In the last case that came to trial, in 1805, Lord Melville, accused of corruption, was acquitted by the Lords in 1806. The next and most recent attempt at impeachment took place in 1848. The Commons debated and rejected charges made against Lord Palmerston, Foreign Secretary at the time, alleging a secret treaty with Russia, as *The Times*[128] reported. Even though this attempt wasn't successful in removing Palmerston, this was due to lack of support for the motion rather than any objection to the use of impeachment as a parliamentary procedure. During their examination of the history of impeachment in Britain, the authors of this report have not come across any mention of the Commons refusing to hear an impeachment.

234. The Palmerston case is of interest today because it concerned making a secret agreement, which is one of the accusations made against the Prime Minister in this report based on accounts by former officials and by journalists. Palmerston survived the attempt at impeachment but he was forced from office a few years later for the same offence of entering into a secret foreign agreement. And this occasion established the precedent that the Foreign Secretary was appointed by the Prime Minister and not directly by the Sovereign – Queen Victoria at that time.

235. The time elapsed since the last impeachment could give the impression that time itself has rendered the procedure obsolete. However, in English history there is a precedent for reviving impeachment after more than a hundred and fifty years; between the 1459 and 1620s.

3.2 The early impeachment trials

236. Impeachment was developed in the fourteenth century at a time when Parliament was growing in power. Initially, the Crown used the House of Lords as a criminal court. In 1376, the Commons first took a prosecution to the Lords, who were the judges. This trial of Richard Lyons and others in 1376 was for financial mismanagement and corruption. From these early years, impeachment was used as a means of enforcing constitutional law and criminal law. The development of the criminal law courts meant that parliament no longer needed to act in such matters. *Hatsell's Precedents*[129] describes how the medieval process of conducting impeachment trials has endured:

> 'The form of proceeding, even in these early instances, particularly in the case of the Duke of Suffolk, in 1450, were much less different from the present, than what at periods so distant might be expected.'

237. A number of royal officials were tried for offences including treason, corruption and maladministration until the time of the Wars of the Roses, when impeachment fell into disuse, the last trial in this period being in 1459. After Henry VII defeated Richard III at Bosworth Field in 1485 and founded the Tudor dynasty, he and his heirs, including Henry VIII and Elizabeth I, established an autocratic style of government which minimised the role of parliament. They took criminal jurisdiction into their own hands in the Court of Star Chamber, so impeachment was not used in the Tudor period except for an unsuccessful attempt to bring Cardinal Woolsey to trial in 1529.

3.3 Impeachment revived in the 1600s to stop absolute monarchy in England

238. In the early 1600s, in the reign of James I, Parliament sought means of legally attacking the King's ministers for subverting the ancient common law of England to the benefit of the King using medieval precedents to assist them. Colin Tite's[130] *Impeachment and Parliamentary Judicature in Early Stuart England* provides a detailed study of the process by which the Stuart Parliaments examined the medieval records. They discovered precedents for conducting impeachment and learnt how the Commons invented new grounds for impeachment in addition to those used by its medieval predecessors. Unlike later trials, during this period impeachment procedures were often completed in weeks.

239. Historically, impeachment is most important for the role it played in establishing parliamentary government in Britain. There is broad agreement amongst constitutional and legal historians that the use of impeachment in England provided the basis for the modern constitution, which holds the power of government accountable to the people through Parliament. Holdsworth describes two critical trials in the 1600s:[131]

> 'The parliamentary opposition in the reigns of the two first Stuart kings was, as we shall see, essentially a legal opposition...It was Buckingham's impeachment which decisively negatived Charles I's contention that not only was he personally above the law, but also his ministers acting under his orders. It was Danby's (under Charles II) which decided that the king could not by use of his power to pardon stop impeachment....The influence of the crown being thus eliminated, impeachments became as the Commons said in 1679, 'the chief institution for the preservation of the government.' Thus, the practice of impeachment has had a large share in establishing English constitutional law upon its modern basis.'

240. Thus, as Holdsworth put it: 'the practice of impeachment has had a large share in establishing English constitutional law upon its modern basis.' Holdsworth goes on to argue that the later use of impeachment as a device to enforce the law became unnecessary because ministers did not act outside of the conventions of the constitution and were compliant with the law. Impeachment's use as a purely political tool also became weak and irrelevant when ministers

could be removed by a vote of no confidence in the House of Commons, an analysis shared by other constitutional and legal historians such as Erskine May:[132]

> 'Impeachment by the Commons, **for high crimes and misdemeanours beyond the reach of the law, or which no other authority in the state will prosecute,** might still be regarded as an ultimate safeguard of public liberty, **though it has not been employed since the beginning of the nineteenth century.**
>
> **Impeachments were directed in particular against Ministers of the Crown; but the growth of the doctrine of collective cabinet responsibility, and of resignation of the cabinet following a successful vote of censure against a minister, resulted in the disuse of impeachments in modern times.'**

and Dicey states:[133]

> **'But though it may be well conceded – and the fact is one of great importance – that** the habit of obedience to the constitution was originally generated and confirmed by impeachments, **they [do not exert] any appreciable influence over the proceedings of the modern statesman…'**

241. Dicey's concludes that impeachment is no longer part of the thinking of ministers and officials. As he puts it:[134]

> *'The arm by which attacks on freedom were once repelled has grown rusty by disuse; it is laid aside among the antiquities of the constitution, nor will it ever, we anticipate, be drawn again from its scabbard.'*

242. Nevertheless, a submission by the present government to the Royal Commission on House of Lords reform makes clear that *the Foreign and Commonwealth Office (FCO) still considers impeachment a current constitutional discipline on ministers.* The following text cited by the FCO in evidence to the Commission is from Halsbury's Laws of England, prepared with FCO assistance:[135]

> 'The relations of ministers of the Crown with foreign powers should be conducted through the proper official and diplomatic channels, and, it seems, be fully disclosed to and open to the criticism and supervision of the Cabinet and of the government as a whole. Deviation from this course on the part of ministers with regard to matters of state exposes their motives to the danger of misinterpretation and is not tolerated by the House of Commons. The danger incurred by a minister who conducts a secret correspondence with foreign powers or agents is clearly shown by the impeachment of the Earl of Danby (see R v Earl of Danby (1685) 11 State Tr 600 at 621-622, HL), where the first article of the impeachment charged him with having "traitorously encroached to himself regal power by treating in matters of peace and war with foreign ministers and ambassadors, and giving instructions to His Majesty's ambassadors abroad without communicating the same to the Secretaries of State and the rest of His Majesty's Council".'

3.4 The eighteenth century – Burke v Hastings and the American copy of impeachment

243. The use of impeachment against the abuse of power and neglect of duty was a feature of the famous case of impeachment against Warren Hastings which took place at the same time as the US Constitution was being written. The prosecution of Hastings by Edmund Burke lasted over a seven-year period and clearly influenced the founders of the US Constitution. A book of essays celebrating the two hundredth anniversary of the trial described it as:[136]

'...a major attempt to institute a public enquiry into the conduct of British officials in a colonial administration, undertaken on clearly stated principles of racial equality and international justice. From the point of view of the managers of the impeachment, states in India were entitled to the same consideration as states in Europe; people in India were entitled to the same protection as people in Britain...An appeal was made to the same assumptions as those that governed the campaign to put an end to the slave trade: all human beings have fundamental legal rights...'

244. As a result of the English origins of US impeachment and its far more recent use in the United States against Richard Nixon in 1974 and Bill Clinton in 1998, most modern analysis of the English history regarding impeachment has been conducted in the United States (Annex C).

245. Many references and discussions of English impeachment relate to the trial of President Clinton. President Clinton's prosecutors argued that the English precedents provided very broad grounds for the impeachment of the President to include his perjury in a private civil case. His defence, however, argued that only crimes affecting the functioning of government and outside the reach of the courts could be considered impeachable.

246. Raoul Berger[137] wrote an authoritative account of impeachment in the US Constitution just before the issue of impeaching Richard Nixon arose. At that time, impeachment had not been used for more that a century in the US and so his study is untainted by any immediate political agenda. He described how:

'...the Founders...referred to the familiar English categories – "subversion of the Constitution" (usurpation of power), "abuse of power", "betrayal of trust", "neglect of duty", and the like.'

3.5 Twentieth century discussions

247. This year the historian Andrew Roberts has argued that in the 1940s a peer of the realm and Admiral of the Fleet should have been impeached on political grounds. Roberts states on his website[138] that:

'In 1994 I published 'Eminent Churchillians'...Each chapter has a very different point to make. 'Lord Mountbatten and the Perils of Adrenalin' makes the case for the impeachment of the last Viceroy of India, on the grounds that his cheating over the India-Pakistan frontier and his headlong rush towards partition led to around one million deaths in Punjab and the North-West Frontier in 1947-48.'

The present Blair government made a case that the parliamentary law of impeachment be abolished by statute.[139]

> 'There are other elements of privilege, which are mainly historical. Freedom from arrest has little application today. Privilege of peerage, which is distinct from parliamentary privilege, still exists although the occasions for its exercise have diminished into obscurity since a peer's right of trial by his peers was abolished in 1948. Even more archaic is impeachment, which has long been in disuse. The 1967 House of Commons select committee on parliamentary privilege recommended that the right to impeach should be formally abandoned and legislation should be introduced for that purpose. The circumstances in which impeachment has taken place are now so remote from the present that the procedure may be considered obsolete.'

248. In direct contrast, Holdsworth concluded his analysis of impeachment by making a strong case for it to be revived with a streamlined procedure. Here he describes a political situation which seems all too familiar:[140]

> 'It [impeachment] does embody the sound principle that ministers and officials should be made criminally liable for corruption, gross negligence, or other misfeances in the conduct of the affairs of the nation. And this principle requires to be emphasised at a time when the development of the system of party government pledges the party to defend the policy of its leaders, however mistaken it may be, and however incompetently it may have been carried out; at a time when party leaders are apt to look indulgently on the most disastrous mistakes, because they hope that the same indulgence will be extended to them when they take office; at a time when the principle of the security of the tenure of higher permanent officials is held to be more important than the need to punish their negligences and ignorances. If ministers were sometimes made criminally responsible for gross negligence or rashness, ill considered activities might be discouraged, real statesmanship might be encouraged and party violence might be moderated.... If officials were sometime made similarly responsible for their errors, it might do something to freshen up that stagnant atmosphere of complacent routine, which is and always has been the most marked characteristic of government departments.'

249. Thus Holdsworth, a twentieth century authority on English legal history, who remains a regular author on university reading lists, firmly recommends the revival of impeachment to ensure effective ministerial accountability.

250. In the meantime, the ability of Parliament to control the activities of government is in continuous decline, consequently public concern is growing. In the current edition of Butterworths textbook, *British Government and the Constitution*,[141] Colin Turpin describes how:

> '...more radical change is needed if the House is to realise the accountability of a government that grows increasingly centralised...The inability, or unwillingness, of the House to call government to account was demonstrated in its passive reaction to the Scott Report (1996), which had revealed serious shortcomings and malpractice in government....Reform should be directed...generally to ways of empowering MPs to press and pursue ministers who are evasive or unwilling to accept responsibility for their actions.'

251. The apparently decreasing power of parliament and the increasing power of government provide the background to considering whether it is appropriate to revive impeachment in relation to the invasion of Iraq.

4. Impeachment as a last resort to hold the Prime Minister to account

252. A Member of Parliament who considers that the Prime Minister is guilty of misconduct or who considers that there is sufficient evidence of a case to answer must now rely on impeachment.

253. Neither of the government enquiries led by Lords Butler and Hutton examined what Menzies Campbell memorably calls the 'flawed prospectus' on which the war was sold to Parliament and the public. Hutton looked very narrowly at the immediate circumstances around the death of Dr David Kelly and the Butler Committee focused on intelligence issues alone.

254. Although various Select Committees have produced reports critical of some aspects of government policy, they have had no effect on the tenure of ministers. Neither have they addressed the overall conduct of the government in relation to the war.

255. The debates in the House of Commons since the attack on Iraq have not centred on the role of the Prime Minister and the government has rejected any further enquiries.

256. If MPs allege that a member of the government has been untruthful in order to create a substantive debate on the issues in question, they are ruled out of order for using unparliamentary language. If they persist they are physically removed from the House. On July 20th 2004, John Baron MP said in the House of Commons:

> 'No, I disagree with that. I think that our Prime Minister, unfortunately, was being pushed by the Americans. That is the centre of the issue. Let us consider the 45-minute claim. That is clear evidence that we as a country were misled by the Prime Minister.'

> Mr. Deputy Speaker: 'Order. That is the second time, I think, that the hon. Gentleman has used that word. He should be very careful with the words he uses. We have strict conventions in the House.'

257. As the Deputy Speaker confirms in the above case, Bagehot's 'modern' 'delicate' means of holding the government to account have been brushed aside as if they did not exist. Impeachment provides the only means of debating serious misconduct within the rules of the House of Commons and, if those who believe it are convincing, remains the only means of prosecuting those concerned.

258. Whereas Erskine May's Parliamentary Proceedings[142] explained that impeachment was no longer needed on the basis that:

> 'the immediate responsibility of the ministers of the Crown to Parliament – the vigilance and activity of that body in scrutinizing the actions of public men'.

259. In respect of the matters described in Chapter 1, Parliament's power has completely broken down. Ministers have not been responsible to Parliament, and Parliament has been neither vigilant nor active.

260. Impeachment is the process by which Parliament can restore its authority and by which public confidence in Parliament may be restored. Impeachment, as Erskine May put it, 'is a safeguard of public liberty well worthy of a free country.'

5. The impeachable offences of the Prime Minister

261. This report concentrates on matters of great public concern, matters where there is strong evidence already and which are most clearly impeachable. These are false and misleading statements and conduct; negligence and incompetence; undermining the constitution; and entering into a secret agreement with a foreign leader. Section 5 also outlines some examples of past impeachments which demonstrate that the historic grounds for impeachment cover the charges against the Prime Minister discussed in this report.

5.1 Misleading Parliament and the country and
failing to resign in consequence

262. Chapter I of this report stipulates the misleading statements and actions of the Prime Minister in his attempt to gain support for invading Iraq, and his subsequent attempts to defend his actions.

263. The history of impeachment and the growth of the constitution show that the constitutional conventions upon which the country relies owe their origins in large part to the discipline imposed by impeachment. The constitutional principle of not lying to Parliament is embodied nowadays in the document 'Questions of procedure for ministers'[143], which states:

> 'Ministers must not knowingly mislead Parliament and the public and should correct any inadvertent errors at the earliest opportunity. They must be as open as possible with Parliament and the public, withholding information only when disclosure would not be in the public interest, which should be decided in accordance with Parliamentary convention, the law and any relevant Government Code of Practice'.

264. Three contemporary examples of the application of these conventions by ministers are the resignations of Beverley Hughes and Peter Mandelson and by the Prime Minister himself in the present government.

265. The detailed accounts explaining why these resignations took place, are discussed in Annex B. The accounts given by the ministers themselves, the Prime Minister and by the Prime Minister's official spokesman all indicate a contemporary consensus on the standards of misleading conduct that require resignation. A reasonable assessment of Chapter 1 of this document leads to the conclusion that the Prime Minister's misleading conduct far exceeded the constitutional standard applied to Ms Hughes and Mr Mandelson. Resignation, in its origins, is a means of avoiding impeachment for misleading conduct, thus it follows that failure to resign leaves the person concerned open to impeachment.

266. Given that the constitution itself has been damaged by the flouting of its laws by the very person whose office is to uphold them, the Prime Minister's failure to resign in the face of overwhelming evidence causes equal offence. This is because the principle of trust on which the relationship between the government and Parliament relies has been weakened, therefore is a charge worthy of impeachment in its own right.

5.2 Negligence and incompetence

267. This report concludes that the Prime Minister was guilty of grave negligence to his office. As illustrated in Chapter I, his culpable offences include:
– not investigating the types of weapons that were supposed to threaten British troops waiting to go into battle against what they were told was an enemy equipped with chemical and biological weapons;
– and for failing to instruct that intelligence reports be provided to assess whether Iraq's final disclosure document was in material breach of UN resolutions so that information was not competently provided to the Attorney General when he was persuaded to certify that an invasion of Iraq would be legal.

268. In 1386, the Duke of Suffolk faced several charges of incompetence that included failing to use the correct machinery of government and incompetently conducting the defence of the country. The specific issues of that time concerned failing to implement prior parliamentary decisions regarding the sale of property and the raising of taxes, and the loss to the French of the city of Ghent.[144] The incompetent conduct of foreign and military policy and negligence in the exercise of office was also a cause of impeachment in the reigns of Charles I, Charles II and, most notably, in the case against Warren Hastings.

269. Nowadays these matters are the subject of normal political debate and politicians and the electorate have the opportunity to debate these issues on television, in the newspapers and ultimately at the ballot box. However, it was only in response to external pressures from outside Parliament, that the Hutton and Butler enquiries were established thus exposing much of our present knowledge about the Iraq affair.

5.3 Undermining the Constitution

270. The Prime Minister undermined the constitution by weakening the machinery of cabinet government. This matter is discussed by Lord Butler as a concern with respect to intelligence matters; however, due to the inquiry's limited terms of reference, the Butler report fails to reach a decisive conclusion. By embarking upon impeachment procedures, Parliament will achieve a broader and deeper examination of the issue.

5.4 Entering into a secret agreement with the President of the United States regarding the overthrow of Saddam Hussein.

271. Chapter I of this report finds that there is strong evidence that the Prime Minister committed his support to President Bush for an invasion of Iraq in 2002.

He did this in the knowledge that the US administration had already decided to oust Saddam Hussein, regardless of any progress on the issue of Iraq's weapons (Chapter I, Section 4).

272. As demonstrated in Chapter I, several distinguished figures state that the Prime Minister had a prior agreement with President Bush to remove Saddam Hussein from power.

273. For the Prime Minister to enter an agreement with a foreign leader without the prior consent or knowledge of Parliament and the Cabinet is impeachable. This is shown in government's own evidence to the Royal Commission on Reform of the House of Lords. The most recent attempt to impeach a minister in 1848 was on similar charges. Thus a successful impeachment on this charge has precedent, and a Commons debate on the subject was secured. For the Prime Minister to have made any substantive agreement regarding US and UK policy towards Iraq without informing his colleagues renders him even more vulnerable to the charge of impeachment.

Useful precedents when considering the conduct of the Prime Minister

274. This section lists some examples of past impeachments which demonstrate that parallels can be drawn between historic cases of impeachment and the charges outlined in this report against the Prime Minister.

1376 Richard Lyons: 'deceit', 4 *Hatsell's Precedents* 50

1386 Earl of Suffolk: Article 1 'deceit', Article 2 negligence, Article 3 dishonesty, Article 5 dishonesty, Article 6 subversion of the law of the King's court, Article 7 negligence in national defence; *Cobbett's Parliamentary History* 188; 1.

1624 Lord Treasurer Middlesex: abuse of power, corruption, negligence; I *Cobbett's Parliamentary History* 1411.

1626 Duke of Buckingham: Article 1 abuse of office 'prejudice of that service that should have been performed in them', Article 2 & 3 abuse of office and dishonesty, Article 4 negligence in national defence, Articles 5, 6 & 7 dishonesty and endangering national defence. Article 11 damaging the honour of the country, Article 12 Abuse of office, 2 *Cobbett's Parliamentary History* 80, 2 *Howell's State Trials* 1268.

1637 Judge Berkley: Article 1 'endeavoured to subvert the fundamental laws and established government of the realm of England', 3 *Howell's State Trials* 1283.

1641 Lord Kimbolton et al: Article 'endeavoured to subvert the fundamental law and Government of this Kingdom.' 2 *Cobbett's Parliamentary History* 1089.

1642 Archbishop Laud: Article 2 'endeavoured to subvert the fundamental laws of this realm; and to that end hath in like manner endeavoured to advance the power of the Council-Table, and the Canons of the Church, and the power of the king's prerogative, above the laws and statutes of the realm.' 2 *Cobbett's Parliamentary History* 1466.

1648 Sir John Maynard: Article 2 & 7 '...subvert the freedom of parliament.' 3 *Cobbett's Parliamentary History* 838.

1668 Peter Pett: 6 *Howell's State Trials* 866 Article 1 negligence in defence of the country.

1673 Henry Bennett: Principal Secretary of State, Article 3 '…betrayed the great trust reposed in him.' 4 *Cobbett's Parliamentary History* 658.

1680 Lord Chief Justice Scroggs and others: Article 1 'subvert the fundamental laws…and government of this kingdom of England.' 4 *Cobbett's Parliamentary History* 1274.

1678 Earl of Danby Lord High Treasurer: Article 1; 'encroached to himself Regal Power, by treating in matters of peace and war with foreign ministers and ambassadors abroad, without communicating the same to secretaries of state, and the rest of his majesty's council.' Article 2 'endeavoured to subvert the ancient and well established form of government in this kingdom.' 4 *Cobbett's Parliamentary History* 693.

1678 Earl of Oxford: Article 1: '…violation of his duty and trust…', Article 2 '…breach of trust…' Articles 6, 7, &8 negligence in defence of the country. 5 *Cobbett's Parliamentary History* 1257.

1701 Lord Somers: Articles 1 to 7 making a secret treaty 'not having first communicated the same to the rest of the ten lords justices of England, or advised in council with his majesty's privy council thereupon.' 2 *Cobbett's Parliamentary History* 1266.

1786 Warren Hastings: various illegal wars, Article 7 '…breach of his duty article 14 breach of his duty…' *Works of Edmund Burke* Vol 3 page 106 (Harper and Bros 1786)

Annex A

Extracts on Impeachment from Erskine May,
Parliamentary Procedure, 1ˢᵗ Edition (p. 374-381)

Impeachment by the Commons; Grounds of Accusation; Form of the Charge; Articles of impeachment; The Trial and Judgment; Proceedings not concluded by Prorogation or Dissolution; Pardon not Pleadable. Trial of Peers. Bills of Attainder and of Pains and Penalties.

Impeachment by the commons, for high crimes and misdemeanours beyond the reach of the law, or which no other authority in the state will prosecute, is a safeguard of public liberty well worthy of a free country, and of so noble an institution as a free Parliament. But, happily, in modern times, this extraordinary judicature is rarely called into activity, the times in which its exercise was needed were those in which the people were jealous of the Crown; when the Parliament had less control over prerogative; when courts of justice were impure; and when, instead of vindicating the law, the Crown and its officers resisted its execution, and screened political offenders from justice, but the limitations of prerogative – the immediate responsibility of the ministers of the Crown to Parliament – the vigilance and activity of that body in scrutinizing the actions of public men – the settled administration of the law, and the direct influence of Parliament over courts of justice – which are, at the same time, independent of the Crown – have prevented the consummation of those crimes which impeachments were designed to punish. The Crown is entrusted by the constitution with the prosecution of all offences; there are few which the law cannot punish; and if the executive officers of the Crown be negligent or corrupt, they are directly amenable to public opinion, and to the censure of Parliament.

From these causes, impeachments are reserved for extraordinary crimes and extraordinary offenders; but by the law of Parliament, all persons, whether peers or commoners, may be impeached for any crimes whatsoever.

It was always allowed, that a peer might be impeached for any crime, whether it were cognizable by the ordinary tribunals or not; but it was formerly doubted, upon the authority of the case of Simon de Beresford, in the *4th Edward 3*, whether a commoner could be impeached for any capital offence.

On the 26th March 1681, Edward Fitzharris was impeached of high treason; but the House of Lords, on being informed by the attorney-general that he had been instructed to indict Fitzharris at common law, resolved that they would not proceed with the impeachment. The grounds of their decision were not stated; but from the protest entered on their Journals, from the resolution of the commons, and from the debates in both houses, it may be collected that the fact of his being a commoner had been mainly relied on. The commons protested against the resolution of the lords, as 'a denial of justice, and a violation of the constitution of Parliaments;' and declared it to be their 'undoubted right to impeach any peer or commoner for treason or any other crime or misdemeanour:' but the impeachment was at an end, and the trial at common law proceeded. On his prosecution by indictment, Fitzharris pleaded in abatement that an impeachment was then pending against him for the same offence, but his plea was overruled by the Court of King's Bench.

The authority of this case, however, is of little value: an impeachment for high treason was pending at the very time against Chief Justice Scroggs, a commoner; and when, on the 26th June 1689, Sir Adam Blair, and four other commoners, were impeached of high treason, the Lords, after receiving a report of precedents, and negativing a motion for requiring the opinion of the judges, resolved that the impeachment should proceed.

It rest, therefore, with the House of Commons to determine when an impeachment should be instituted. A member, in his place, first charges the accused of high treason, or of certain high crimes and misdemeanours, and after supporting his charge with proofs, moves that he be impeached. If the house deem the grounds of accusation sufficient, and agree to the motion, the member is ordered to go to the lords, 'and at their bar, in the name of the House of Commons, and of all the commons of the United Kingdom, to impeach the accused; and to acquaint them that this house will, in due time, exhibit particular articles against him, and make good the same.' The member, accompanied by several others, proceeds to the bar of the House of Lords, and impeaches the accused accordingly.

In the case of Warren Hastings, articles of impeachment had been prepared before his formal impeachment at the bar of the House of Lords; but the usual course has been to prepare them afterwards. A committee is appointed to draw up the articles, and on their report, the articles are discussed, and, when agreed to, are engrossed and delivered to the lords, with a saving clause, to provide that the commons shall be at liberty to exhibit further articles from time to time. The accused sends answers to each article, which, together with all writings delivered in by him, are communicated to the commons by the lords; and to these replications are returned if necessary.

If the accused be a peer, he is attached or retained in custody by order of the House of Lords; if a commoner, he is taken into custody by the serjeant-at-arms attending the commons, by whom he is delivered to the gentleman usher of the black rod, in whose custody he remains, unless he be admitted to bail by the House of Lords; or be otherwise disposed of by their order.

The lords appoint a day for the trial, and in the meantime the commons appoint managers to prepare evidence and conduct the proceedings, and desire the lords to summon all witnesses who are required to prove their charges. The accused may have summonses issued for the attendance of witnesses on his behalf, and is entitled to make his full defence by counsel.

The trial has usually been held in Westminster Hall, which has been fitted up for that purpose. In the case of peers impeached of high treason, the House of Lords is presided over the lords high steward, who is appointed by the Crown, on the address of their lordships; but, at other times, by the lord chancellor or lord speaker of the House of Lords. The commons attend the trial, as a committee of the whole house, when the managers make their charges, and adduce evidence in support of them; but they are bound to confine themselves to charges contained in the articles of impeachment. Mr Warren Hastings complained, by petition to the House of Commons, that matters of accusation had been added to those originally laid to his charge, and the house resolved that certain words ought not to have been spoken by Mr Burke. When the case has been completed by the managers, they are answered by the counsel for the accused, by whom witnesses are also examined, if necessary; and, in conclusion, the managers have a right of reply.

When the case is thus concluded, the lords proceed to determine whether the accused be guilty of the crimes with which he has been charged, the lord high steward puts to each peer, beginning with the junior baron, the question upon the first article, whether the accused be guilty of the crimes charged therein. The peers in succession rise in their places when the question is put, and standing uncovered, and laying their right hands upon their breasts, answer, 'guilty', or 'not guilty', as the case may be, 'upon my honour'. Each article is proceeded with separately in the same manner, the lord high steward giving his own opinion the last. The numbers are then cast up, and being ascertained, are declared by the lord high steward to the lords, and the accused is acquainted with the result.

If the accused be declared not guilty, the impeachment is dismissed; but if guilty, it is for the commons, in the first place, to demand judgment of the lords against him; without which they would protest against any judgment being pronounced. On the 17th March 1715, the commons resolved, nem con, in the impeachment of the Earl of Winton,

'That the managers for the commons be empowered, in case the House of Lords shall proceed to judgment before the same is demanded by the commons, to insist upon it, that it is not parliamentary for their lordships to give judgement, until the same be first demanded by this house.'

And a similar resolution was agreed to on the impeachment of Lord Lovat, in 1746.

When judgment is to be given, the lords send a message to acquaint the commons that their lordships are ready to proceed further upon the impeachment; the managers attend; and the accused, being called to the bar, is then permitted to offer matters in arrest of judgment. Judgment is afterwards demanded by the speaker, in the name of the commons, and pronounced by the lord high steward, the Lord Chancellor, or speaker of the House of Lords.

The necessity of demanding judgment gives to the commons the power of pardoning the accused, after he has been found guilty by the lords; and in this manner an attempt was made, in 1725, to save the Earl of Macclesfield from the consequences of an impeachment, after he had been found guilty by the unanimous judgment of the House of Lords.

So important is an impeachment by the commons, that not only does it continue from session to session, in spite of prorogations, by which all other parliamentary proceedings are determined; but it survives even a dissolution, by which the very existence of a Parliament is concluded. But as the preliminary proceedings of the House of Commons would require to be revived in another session, Acts were passed in 1786 and in 1805, to provide that the proceedings depending in the House of Commons upon the articles of charge against Warren Hastings and Lord Melville, should not be discontinued by nay prorogation or dissolution of Parliament.

In the case of the Earl of Danby, in 1679, the commons protested against a royal pardon being pleaded in bar of an impeachment, by which an offender could be screened from the inquiry and justice of Parliament by the intervention of prerogative. Directly after the Revolution, the commons asserted the same principle, and within a few years, it was declared by the Act of Settlement, 'That no pardon under the great seal of England shall be pleadable to an impeachment by the commons in Parliament.'

But, although the royal prerogative of pardon is not suffered to obstruct the course of justice, and to interfere with the exercise of parliamentary judicature; yet the prerogative itself is unimpaired in regard to all convictions whatever; and therefore, after the judgment of the lords has been pronounced, the Crown may reprieve or pardon the offender. This right was exercised in the case of three of the Scottish lords, who had been concerned in the rebellion of 1715, and who were reprieved by the Crown, and at length received the royal pardon. Concerning the trial of peers, very few words will be necessary.

Annex B

The constitutional standard for ministerial resignation for misleading conduct in the cases of Ms Hughes and Mr Mandelson

Chapter 1 of this report is a catalogue of statements by the Prime Minister that are contradicted by the very sources that the statements purport to rely on, yet no action is proposed either from within the cabinet on which the constitution depends to control the Prime Minister or from her Majesty's opposition. The normal conventions of the constitution would require resignation if only a fraction of the improprieties we catalogue were valid. Compare them to the standard applied by the Prime Minister and the official opposition to the resignations of Ms Beverley Hughes MP and Mr Peter Mandelson MP.

B.1 The following is an extract from the statement made by the Prime Minister's Official Spokesman concerning the resignation of Ms Hughes. [145]

'In answer to questions, the Prime Minister's Official Spokesman (PMOS) said it was important to be clear that the concerns raised by Bob Ainsworth were of a different order to the allegations – as yet unproven – which had been expressed in recent days. Those allegations centred on the suggestion that there was a policy to approve fraudulent documents knowingly. That was obviously a more serious claim than some of the concerns expressed by Mr Ainsworth. Of course that was not to suggest that his concerns were negligible. They were not, as Ms Hughes had shown by responding to his letter last March. Clearly Ken Sutton would look at the substance of the claims. Questioned as to why, if that was the case, Ms Hughes had resigned as a result of Mr Ainsworth's concerns rather than the allegations which had been made earlier in the week, the PMOS said that the question was based on a misunderstanding. Having subsequently seen the papers – of which she had clearly had no recollection when doing interviews on Monday evening – **Ms Hughes felt that she might have given a misleading impression that this was the first time that general concerns about Romania had been raised with her. She had been accurate to say that it was the first time the specific allegations relating to fraud, as had been reported over the last few days, had been raised with her. However, it was wrong to have given the impression that other concerns had not been raised, as clearly they had.** Asked again, the PMOS said it was important to be clear that there were two different issues here: concerns expressed by Bob Ainsworth and allegations – as yet unproven – relating to systematic fraud which had been raised earlier this week. **In saying that she hadn't heard about those allegations, she believed that she had unwittingly given the impression that she hadn't heard about any concerns regarding Romania, when in fact she had from Bob Ainsworth. That was why she had resigned.**'

Ms Hughes's explanation on the matter in the House of Commons was:[146]

'I am confident that at all times I have acted properly and in the best interests of the people of this country, and I am proud of what I have achieved over the past two years. None the less, it has become clear to me that, however unwittingly, **I may have given**

a misleading impression in my interviews on Monday night about whether any of the concerns expressed about the operation of clearance controls from Romania and Bulgaria had crossed my desk at any stage in the past two years.'

'On Tuesday, in order to prepare for the next phase of the Sutton inquiry, I asked for all the relevant files and paperwork to be reviewed in order to ensure that everything was correctly disclosed. During this process it was discovered that my hon. Friend the Member for Coventry, North-East (Mr. Ainsworth) had written to me a year ago drawing my attention to pro forma business plans submitted by UK solicitors in Romanian and Bulgarian cases. I did, in fact, take action at that time on advice from officials to address those concerns. I realised that that was what my hon. Friend was referring to when he mentioned that correspondence to me briefly in the Lobby.'

'On Wednesday, having re-read the interviews that I gave on Monday, **I realised that what I said then was not fully consistent with that correspondence. Once the full picture was clear to me, I asked to see both the Prime Minister and the Home Secretary to explain that I had decided that I could not continue.** I have always said that in my political and my personal life nothing is more important than my integrity, and although I did not intentionally mislead anyone I have decided that I cannot in conscience continue to serve as immigration Minister.'

In summary, Ms Hughes said, and the Prime Minister accepted, that the fact that she had unintentionally given the impression that she had not known something that she had in fact known was reason for to resign. We can find no reason to consider the statements of the Prime Minister detailed in Chapter 1 of this report as being any less misleading than the actions of Ms Hughes and every reason to assess them as of incomparably greater significance.

B.2 The second resignation of Peter Mandelson MP also makes clear the normal standard of accuracy required for a minister to remain in office. This is Mr Mandelson's own statement on why he resigned in January 2001.[147]

'I am today resigning from the government and wish to set out the background to my decision.

I do not accept in any way that I have acted improperly in respect of any application for naturalisation as a British subject.

I do accept, however, that **when my office spoke to a Sunday newspaper at the weekend, I should have been clear that it was me personally, not my official, who spoke to the Home Office minister.**

As a result of that reply, incorrect information was given to the House by the culture secretary and to the Press by the prime minister's official spokesman.

I accept responsibility for that. I have said to the prime minister that I wish to leave the government and he has accepted that.

I would only ask people to understand that my sole desire and motivation throughout was to emphasise that I had not sought to influence the decision on naturalisation in any way at all, merely to pass on a request for information and the prime minister is entirely satisfied with this.

I confess in reaching my decision, that there is another factor.

As a reading of today's newspapers shows all too graphically, there must be more to politics than the constant media pressure and exposure that has dogged me over the last five or so years.

I want to remove myself from the countless stories of controversy, of feuds of divisions and all the rest, all the other stories that have surrounded me.

I want in other words, to lead a more normal life, both in politics and in the future outside.

That is my decision and I hope that everyone will understand and respect it.

Finally it has been the greatest privilege of my political life to play a part in the peace process in Northern Ireland, something far bigger and more important that any one individual or his career.

We are so close now to a final settlement, to a complete implementation of this government's, as well as others' achievement, the Good Friday Agreement.

I only hope and pray that everything that we have worked for and the parties in Northern Ireland have worked for now comes to pass and I wish the people in Northern Ireland every success and peace in the future and I thank them for their kindness to me.

The prime minister has asked me to do Northern Ireland questions in the House this afternoon. I shall then listen to Prime Minister's questions and then formally I will resign from the government.'

The Prime Minister's official spokesman explained the matter in this way:[148]

'Questioned about the Prime Minister's meeting with Peter Mandelson this morning, the PMOS said that in light of the fact that PMQs had been due to take place this afternoon, the Prime Minister had wanted to sit down and go through the whole thing with Mr Mandelson. There were two parts to this story. First, the issue of the application by Mr Hinduja. As the Prime Minister had said this afternoon, he was satisfied that the application had been handled properly and according to the relevant and appropriate criteria. Nonetheless, he wanted Sir Anthony Hammond to have a look at the application. Sir Anthony had agreed to do so as soon as he was available. The second part of the story related to the account of it over the past few days. **On this point, Mr Mandelson had acknowledged and volunteered that the account that had been given to us – which we had passed on and which Chris Smith had relied upon when speaking to the Commons on Monday – had been wrong and he had accepted responsibility for that.**

Asked whether Peter Mandelson could have held on to his job or whether the Prime Minister had decided he should resign, **the PMOS repeated that the Prime Minister had wanted to go through all the facts of the case with Mr Mandelson this morning and that was what he had done.** Asked for details of the meeting, the PMOS said that it had started at 10.45am. It had lasted over an hour and had taken place in the Prime Minister's office. Asked who else had been present, the PMOS said that it had just been the Prime Minister and Mr Mandelson for the bulk of the meeting. Others had been involved as required. People had been speculating as to why Mr Mandelson had remained in Downing Street for so long. The reason was because there were other things going on, although not all involving the Prime Minister. For example, there had been discussions about how Mr Mandelson's resignation would be announced, a discussion about whether it was appropriate for him to take questions on Northern Ireland in the House as the Prime Minister had wanted him to do and we had also been trying to contact Sir Anthony Hammond. In addition, Mr Mandelson had been preparing for Northern Ireland Questions in the House.

Questioned about Peter Mandelson's comments in an interview last night that no one had asked him about his conversation with Mike O'Brien, the PMOS said that Mr Mandelson's office had dealt with this point last night. He added reports that there had been some terrible row between him and Mr Mandelson were inaccurate. It had not been like that at all. **The Prime Minister, in a focussed way, had been seeking to get to the bottom of the facts as they were available to us. It was clear that the facts which had been made available to us had not been consistent – a fact that Mr Mandelson had acknowledged. Mr Mandelson had also acknowledged that what had happened over the last few days was not acceptable.**

Asked if Mr Mandelson had explained why he had lied on three separate counts – to The Observer, to the PMOS and to the House through Chris Smith, the PMOS pointed out that Chris Smith had been relying on what he (the PMOS) had said and the line being deployed at the time. Today Mr Smith had put down a PQ to correct what he had said. The Prime Minister, the Government and Downing Street had been involved in this matter to resolve the situation. It had been resolved in the way that was now widely known. **Mr Mandelson had acknowledged that the account he had given had been misleading. Asked whether it had been deliberate, the PMOS said that, as the journalists had been chronicling, there had been difficulties and inconsistencies.** ....

Asked if Mr Mandelson had given him an explanation as to why he had misled him, the PMOS said he had no intention of going into detail on every conversation that had taken place. We had been open and upfront as much as possible throughout this whole episode. Pressed, the PMOS said that he had relied on Mr Mandelson's recollection as it had been given. That related to the enquiries we had received over the last four days. He had nothing further to add to what he had already said. Asked if the Prime Minister had been influenced by the media coverage of the matter this morning, the PMOS said no. It was obvious yesterday that there were difficulties and inconsistencies in this whole episode. **The Prime Minister had been occupied on Monday and Tuesday with Northern Ireland matters. Obviously he had been aware that it had been an evolving and developing situation. He had started to get as deep into the detail as he could when he began preparing for PMQs yesterday.** Asked about the terms of reference for the Hammond inquiry, the PMOS said that it was 'to establish what approaches were made to the Home Office in 1998 in connection with the possibility of an application for naturalisation by Mr S P Hinduja and the full circumstances surrounding such approaches and the later grant of that application and to report to the Prime Minister...'.

In the House of Commons, Tony Blair explained why he had accepted Mr Mandelson's resignation:[149]

The Prime Minister (Mr. Tony Blair): As the House is well aware, I had a meeting this morning with my right hon. Friend the Secretary of State for Northern Ireland, who has since announced his decision to resign from the Government later today. I would like to pay the warmest possible tribute to him for the tireless efforts he has made to secure peace in Northern Ireland – [Hon. Members: 'Hear, hear.'] – and also for his personal courage and sense of duty in coming to the House this afternoon to answer questions on Northern Ireland before departing the Government.

Mr. Cash: Will the Prime Minister take the opportunity of this Question Time to spell out the truth to the House of Commons and to the country regarding the events surrounding the Secretary of State for Northern Ireland?

The Prime Minister: I accept that the reply of the Secretary of State, through his office, to inquiries from a newspaper at the weekend was misleading and resulted in the House of Commons and the Lobby being misled – and I accepted his resignation on that basis.

On the information presently available to me, I believe that the application for naturalisation of the individual in question was decided in accordance with the proper criteria – and so does the Home Secretary. None the less, I have asked Sir Anthony Hammond QC, former Treasury Solicitor, to review the case fully so that we can be sure that the application was dealt with properly in all respects. Sir Anthony will report his findings to me and we will publish them.

Mr. William Hague (Richmond, Yorks): 24 Jan 2001: Column 916

….Now that the Prime Minister has notched up the historic achievement of being forced to sack the same Minister for the same offence twice in 25 months, does he recognise that his career-long dependency on the right hon. Member for Hartlepool (Mr. Mandelson) has been a monumental error of judgment?

The Prime Minister: I do not suppose that I ever expected the right hon. Gentleman to behave graciously at all on the resignation of my right hon. Friend, but I say to the right hon. Gentleman and to the House that I believe that the job done by my right hon. Friend in Northern Ireland well merited his position as Secretary of State for Northern Ireland. I think he has made an enormous contribution to it; indeed, it is not an exaggeration to say that I doubt whether the process in Northern Ireland would have been sustained so well but for his commitment. I therefore believe it was right that he occupied that position, and I also believe that he is a bigger man than many of his critics.

Mr. Hague: The fact is that to reappoint in September 1999 a disgraced Minister 10 months after he was forced to resign, in breach of every convention and precedent, was a demonstration of the arrogance with which the Prime Minister wields his power. To spare himself and the country going through this a third time, will the Prime Minister now guarantee that his right hon. Friend the Member for Hartlepool will not be running the election campaign of the Labour party and will not return to office in any Government led by him?

The Prime Minister: My right hon. Friend has already made that clear in the statement that he gave earlier. **I simply say to the right hon. Gentleman that I think my right hon. Friend has done the right thing; I think that he has done the honourable thing. It is a long tradition in this House that when someone does that, we pay tribute to it. I am only sorry that once again the Leader of the Opposition has lived down to my expectations**.

Mr. Hague: The right hon. Member for Hartlepool has done the right thing, but it is a pity that the Prime Minister's judgment led him to have to do it twice within the space of one Parliament. Does this not go wider than the matter of the right hon. Gentleman, because he has been central to everything that the Prime Minister has done? It was the right hon. Gentleman who picked the Prime Minister out; the right hon. Gentleman who briefed the press for him; the right hon. Gentleman who stabbed the Chancellor in the back for him; the right hon. Gentleman who spun all of his campaigns for him. Is not the fact that the right hon. Gentleman's statement sadly could not be relied upon the reason not only that he has had to go, but that he has been at the heart of the entire new Labour project?

The Prime Minister: I think the Leader of the Opposition probably wrote most of that before my right hon. Friend resigned; he just forgot to change the script. I repeat that I believe it was right that my right hon. Friend came back into Government as the Secretary of State for Northern Ireland. I honestly believe that, in the broad sweep of history, his contribution to that process will be far greater than what has happened in the past 24 hours, tragic though that is.

Mr. Hague: This is not about the broad sweep of history; it is about the conduct of the Government – the disgraceful conduct – of the Government. Has this not told us everything we need to know, not about the right hon. Member for Hartlepool but about the way in which the Government do their business? The Prime Minister said that they would be purer than pure and, as with every other pledge, he has failed to deliver. When asked to choose between high standards of government and the low politics of his cronies, he has unerringly chosen the latter. He has set those standards himself. In every incomplete answer in the House, in every distorted accusation and in every piece of baseless spin, the Prime Minister has set the standards of the Government. In a Government where standards of truth, honesty and integrity have taken second place to spin and smear, is he not truly the first among equals?

The Prime Minister: I really think that by that performance the right hon. Gentleman diminishes himself far more than he diminishes anybody else – *[Interruption.]* I believe that. **I made it clear that if people did something wrong, they would pay the penalty; and my right hon. Friend has paid the penalty – that is true.** I also believe that he can be very proud of his record and the contribution that he made while he was in Government. As for the rest of the nonsense the Leader of the Opposition has spoken, I have no intention of getting into it.

Again, examine the values expressed in the exchange of letters between Mr Mandelson and Mr Blair on the occasion of Mr Mandelson's first resignation and the actions of the Prime Minister, and indeed some of his officials concerning the case made against Saddam Hussein.

Text of correspondence between Peter Mandelson and Tony Blair following the minister's 1998 resignation:[150]

Thursday December 24, 1998

Dear Tony,
I can scarcely believe I am writing this letter to you. As well as being one of my closest friends you are a close colleague whose leadership and political qualities I value beyond all others.

As you have, I have reflected overnight on the situation concerning the loan I took from Geoffrey Robinson and I have decided to resign from the Government.

As I said publicly yesterday, I do not believe that I have done anything wrong or improper. But **I should not, with all candour, have entered into the arrangement. I should, having done so, told you and other colleagues whose advice I value. And I should have told my permanent secretary on learning**

of the inquiry into Geoffrey Robinson, although I had entirely stood aside from this.

I am sorry about this situation. But **we came to power promising to uphold the highest possible standards in public life. We have not just to do so, but we must be seen to do so.**

Therefore with huge regret I wish to resign. I am very proud of the role I played in helping you and previous leaders of the Labour Party to make our party electable and to win our historic victory last May.

I am proud of the trust you placed in me both at the Cabinet Office and at the DTI. In just 18 months you have helped to transform this country and the government has made huge progress delivering on our manifesto and its programme of modernisation.

I will always be a loyal Labour man and I am not prepared to see the party and the government suffer the kind of attack this issue has provoked.

You can be assured, of course, of my continuing friendship and total loyalty.

Yours ever, Peter.'

Tony Blair's response:

'Dear Peter,

You will know better than anyone the feelings with which I write to you. You and I have been personal friends and the closest of political colleagues.

It is no exaggeration to say that without your support and advice we would never have built New Labour.

It was typical of you, when we spoke last night, that your thought was for the reputation of the Labour party and the government and that you believed that since there had been a misjudgment on your part, then, as you said to me 'we can't be like the last lot' and that what we are trying to achieve for the country is more important than any individual.

But I also want you to know that you have my profound thanks for all you have done and my belief that, in the future, you will achieve much, much more with us.

Yours ever, Tony.'

Mr Mandelson resigned on the first occasion because he failed to disclose information to the appropriate officials about a personal financial transaction that he should not have made in th first place. On the second occasion he made misleading statements and caused others to make misleading statements on his behalf. Ms Hughes forgot she knew something and said she did not know it. It is not reasonable to conclude that the matters discussed in Chapter 1 of this report are less misleading actions and statement than those of Mr Mandelson and Ms Hughes.

Annex C

**Extracts from the report of the Judiciary Committee of the
US House of Representatives on Constitutional Grounds for
Presidential Impeachment, 1974**

The English Parliamentary Practice

Alexander Hamilton wrote, in No. 65 of *The Federalist*, that Great Britain had served as 'the model from which [impeachment] has been borrowed.' Accordingly, its history in England is useful to an understanding of the purpose and scope of the impeachment in the United States.

Parliament developed the impeachment as a means to exercise some measure of control over the King. An impeachment proceeding in England was a direct method of bringing into account the King's ministers and favourites – men who might have otherwise been out of reach. Impeachment, at least in its early history, has been called 'the most powerful weapon in the political armoury, short of civil war.'[151] It played a continuing role in the struggles between King and Parliament that resulted in the formation of the unwritten English constitution. In this respect impeachment was one of the tools used by English Parliament to create more responsive and responsible government and to redress imbalances when they occurred.[152]

The long struggle by Parliament to assert legal restraints over the unbridled will of the King ultimately reached a climax with the execution of Charles I in 1649 and the establishment of the Commonwealth under Oliver Cromwell. In the course of that struggle, Parliament sought to exert restraints over the King by removing those of his ministers who most effectively advanced the King's absolutist purposes. Chief among them was Thomas Wentworth, Earl of Strafford. The House of Commons impeached him in 1640. As with earlier impeachments, the thrust of the charges was damage to the state.[153] The first article of impeachment alleged[154]

> That he . hath traitorously endeavoured to subvert the Fundamental Laws and Government of the Realms . . . and in stead thereof, to introduce Arbitrary and Tyrannical Government against Law . . .

The other articles against Strafford included charges ranging from the allegation that he had assumed regal power and exercised it tyrannically to the charge that he subverted the rights of Parliament.[155]

Characteristically, impeachment was used in individual cases to reach offenses, as perceived by Parliament, against the system of government. The charges, variously denominated 'treason,' 'high treason,' 'misdemeanors,' 'malversations,' and high Crimes and Misdemeanors,' thus included allegations of misconduct as various as the kings (or their ministers) were ingenious in devising means of expanding royal power.

At the time of the Constitutional Convention the phrase 'high Crimes and Misdemeanors' had been in use for over 400 years in impeachment proceedings in Parliament.[156] It first appears in 1386 in the impeachment of the King's Chancellor. Michael de le Pole, Earl of Suffolk.[157] Some of the charges may have involved common law offenses.[158] Others plainly did not: de la Pole was charged with breaking a promise he made to the full Parliament to execute in connection with a parliamentary ordinance the advice of a committee of nine lords regarding the improvement of the estate of the King and the realm: 'this was not done, and it was the fault of himself as he was then chief officer.' He was also charged with failing to expend a sum that Parliament had directed be used to ransom the town of Ghent, because of which 'the said town was lost.'[159]

The phrase does not reappear in impeachment proceedings until 1450. In that year articles of impeachment against William de la Pole, Duke of Suffolk (a descendant of Michael), charged him with several acts of high treason, but also with 'high Crimes and Misdemeanors,'[160] including such various offences as 'advising the King to grant liberties and privileges to certain persons to the hindrance of the due execution of the laws,' 'procuring offices for person who were unfit , and unworthy of them' and 'squandering away the public treasure.'[161]

Impeachment was used frequently during the reigns of James I (1603-1625) and Charles I (1628-1649). During the period from 1620 to 1649 over 100 impeachments were voted by the House of Commons.[162] Some of these impeachments charged high treason, as in the case of Strafford; others charged high crimes and misdemeanors. The latter included both statutory offences, particularly with respect to the Crown monopolies and non-statutory offences. For example, Sir Henry Yelverton, the King's Attorney General, was impeached in 1621 of high crimes and misdemeanors in that he failed to prosecute after commencing suits, and exercised authority before it was properly vested in him.[163]

There were no impeachments during the Commonwealth (1649-1660). Following the end of the Commonwealth and the Restoration of Charles II (1660-1685) a more powerful Parliament expanded somewhat the scope of 'high Crimes and Misdemeanors' by the impeaching officers of the Crown for such things as negligent discharge of duties[164] and improprieties in office.[165]

The phrase 'high Crimes and Misdemeanors' appears in nearly all of the comparatively few impeachments that occurred in the eighteenth century. Many of the charges involved abuse of official power or trust. For example, Edward, Earl of Oxford, was charged in 1701 with 'violation of his duty and trust' in that, while a member of the King's privy council, he took advantage of the ready access he had to the King to secure various royal rents and revenues for his own use, thereby greatly diminishing the revenues of the crown and subjecting the people of England to 'grievous taxes.'[166] Oxford was also charged with procuring a naval commission for William Kidd, 'known to be a person of ill fame and reputation,' and ordering him 'to pursue the intended voyage, in which Kidd did commit diverse piracies…, being thereto encourage through hopes of being protected by the high station and interest of Oxford, in violation of the laws of nations, and the interruption and discouragement of the trade of England.'[167]

The impeachment of Warren Hastings, first attempted in 1786 and concluded in 1795,[168] is particularly important because [it was] contemporaneous with the American Convention debates. Hastings was the first Governor-General of India. The articles indicate that Hastings was being charged with high crimes and misdemeanors in the form of gross maladministration, corruption in office, and cruelty toward the people of India.[169]

Two points emerge from the 400 years of English parliamentary experience with the phrase 'high Crimes and Misdemeanors.' First the particular allegations of misconduct alleged damage to the state in such forms as misapplication of funds, abuse of official power, neglect of duty, encroachment on Parliament's prerogatives, corruption, and betrayal of trust.[170] Second, the phrase 'high Crimes and Misdemeanors' was confined to parliamentary impeachments; it had no roots in the ordinary criminal law,[171] and the particular allegations of misconduct under that heading were not necessarily limited to common law or statutory derelictions or crimes.

Conclusion

Impeachment is a constitutional remedy addressed to serious offences against the system of government. The purpose of impeachment under the Constitution is indicated by the limited scope of the remedy (removal from office and possible disqualification from future office) and by the stated grounds for impeachment (treason, bribery, and other high crimes and misdemeanors). It is not controlling whether treason and bribery are criminal. More important, they are constitutional wrongs that subvert the structure of government, or undermine the integrity of office and even the Constitution itself, and thus are 'high' offences in the sense that word was used in English impeachments.

The framers of our Constitution conspicuously adopted a particular phrase from the English practice to help define the constitutional grounds for removal. The content of the phrase 'high Crimes and Misdemeanors' for the framers is to be related to what the framers knew, on the whole, about the English practice – the broad sweep of English constitutional history and the vital role impeachment had played in the limitation of royal prerogative and the control of abuses of ministerial and judicial power.

Impeachment was not a remote subject for the framers. Even as they labored in Philadelphia, the impeachment trial of Warren Hastings, Governor-General of India, was pending in London, a fact to which George Mason made explicit reference in the Convention. Whatever may be said on the merits of Hastings' conduct, the charges against him exemplified the central aspect of impeachment – the parliamentary effort to reach grave abuses of governmental power.

The framers understood quite clearly that the constitutional system they were creating must include some ultimate check on the conduct of the executive, particularly as they came to reject the suggested plural executive. While insistent that balance between the executive and legislative branches be maintained so that the executive would not become the creature of the legislature, dismissible at its will, the framers also recognized that some means would be needed to deal with excesses by the executive. Impeachment was familiar to them. They understood its essential constitutional functions and perceived its adaptability to the American contest.

While it may be argued that some articles of impeachment have charged conduct that constituted crime and thus that criminality is an essential ingredient, or that some have charged conduct that was not criminal and thus that criminality is not essential, the fact remains that in the English practice and in several of the American impeachments the criminality issue was not raised at all. The emphasis has been on the significant effects of the conduct – undermining the integrity of office, disregard of constitutional duties and oath of office, arrogation of power, abuse of the governmental process, adverse impact on the system of government. Clearly, these effects can be brought about in ways not anticipated by the criminal law. Criminal standards and criminal courts were established to control individual conduct. Impeachment was evolved by Parliament to cope with both the inadequacy of criminal standards and the impotence of courts to deal with the conduct of great public figures. It would be anomalous if the framers, having barred criminal sanctions from the impeachment remedy and limited it to removal and possible disqualification from office, intended to restrict the grounds for impeachment to conduct that was criminal.

The longing for precise criteria is understandable; advance, precise definition of objective limits would seemingly serve both to direct future conduct and to inhibit arbitrary reaction to past conduct. In private affairs the objective is the control of personal behaviour, in part through the punishment of misbehaviour. In general, advance definition of standards respecting private conduct works reasonably well. However, where the issue is presidential compliance with the constitutional requirements and limitations on the presidency, the crucial factor is not the intrinsic quality of behaviour but the significance of its effect upon our constitutional system or the functioning of our government.

It is useful to note three major presidential duties of broad scope that are explicitly recited in the Constitution: 'to take Care that the Laws be faithfully executed,' to 'faithfully execute the Office of President of the United States' and to 'preserve, protect, and defend the Constitution of the United States' to the best of his ability. The first is directly imposed by the Constitution; the second and third are included in the constitutionally prescribed oath that the President is required to take before he enters upon the execution of his office and are, therefore, also expressly imposed by the Constitution.

The duty to take care is affirmative. So is the duty faithfully to execute the office. A President must carry out the obligations of his office diligently and in good faith. The elective character and political role of a President make it difficult to define faithful exercise of his powers in the abstract. A President must make policy and exercise discretion. This discretion necessarily is broad, especially in emergency situations, but the constitutional duties of a President impose limitations on its exercise.

The 'take care' duty emphasizes the responsibility of a President for the overall conduct of the executive branch, which the Constitution vests in him alone. He must take care that the executive is so organized and operated that this duty is performed.

The duty of a President to 'preserve, protect, and defend the Constitution' to the best of his ability includes the duty not to abuse his powers or transgress their limits – not to violate the rights of citizens, such as those guaranteed by the Bill of Rights, and not to act in derogation of powers elsewhere by the Constitution.

Not all presidential misconduct is sufficient to constitute grounds for impeachment. There is further requirement – substantiality. In deciding whether this further requirement has been met, the facts must be considered as a whole in the context of the office, not in terms of separate or isolated events. Because impeachment of a President is a grave step for the nation, it is predicated only upon conduct seriously incompatible with either the constitutional form and principles of our government or the proper performance of constitutional duties of the presidential office.

Chapter I References

1 Transcript available on the Downing Street website, at: http://www.number-10.gov.uk/output/Page1727.asp. Emphasis in this report has been added, unless otherwise noted.

2 Quoted in, *inter alia*, *The Times*, 4 March 2002.

3 http://www.number-10.gov.uk/output/Page1704.asp

4 http://www.number-10.gov.uk/output/Page1709.asp

5 http://www.pm.gov.uk/output/Page1711.asp

6 Hansard, 10 April 2002, col. 23.

7 Annex B of the Butler report, pp.164, 167, 168-69.

8 Hansard, 10 April 2002, cols. 11 and 23.

9 http://www.number-10.gov.uk/output/Page3001.asp

10 http://www.number-10.gov.uk/output/Page1725.asp

11 http://www.number-10.gov.uk/output/Page1770.asp

12 http://www.number-10.gov.uk/output/Page3088.asp

13 Hansard, 18 March 2003, col. 760.

14 Butler report, §261.

15 Butler report, §291.

16 Annex B of the Butler report, p.164, column 2.

17 Butler report, §334.

18 Draft dossier of 19 September 2002, p.19; at http://www.the-hutton-inquiry.org.uk/content/cab/cab_3_0022to0078.pdf

19 Intelligence and Security Committee, Iraqi Weapons of Mass Destruction – Intelligence and Assessments, September 2003, §111.

20 http://www.the-hutton-inquiry.org.uk/content/cab/cab_11_0047to0048.pdf

21 http://www.the-hutton-inquiry.org.uk/content/cab/cab_11_0069.pdf

22 UNSCOM report of January 1999, Appendix III, at: http://www.un.org/Depts/unscom/s99-94.htm

23 http://www.number-10.gov.uk/output/Page1725.asp

24 http://www.number-10.gov.uk/output/Page3088.asp

25 http://www.number-10.gov.uk/output/Page3294.asp

26 Briefing of the Security Council, 14 February 2003, at:
http://www.un.org/apps/news/infocusnewsiraq.asp?NewsID=382&sID=6

27 JIC Assessment of 15 March 2002, in Annex B of the Butler report, p.167, column 1.

28 http://www.publications.parliament.uk/pa/cm200102/cmselect/cmliaisn/1095/2071607.htm

29 http://www.pm.gov.uk/output/Page1725.asp

30 http://www.number-10.gov.uk/output/Page1727.asp

31 Butler report, §261.

32 Quoted in the Butler report, §384.

33 http://www.number-10.gov.uk/output/Page3088.asp

34 'The Status of Nuclear Inspections in Iraq: 14 February 2003 Update', at:
http://www.iaea.org/NewsCenter/Statements/2003/ebsp2003n005.shtml

35 Briefing of the Security Council, 14 February 2003, at:
http://www.un.org/apps/news/infocusnewsiraq.asp?NewsID=382&sID=6

36 Oral introduction of the 12th quarterly report of UNMOVIC, 7 March 2003, at:
http://www.un.org/Depts/unmovic/SC7asdelivered.htm

37 http://www.number-10.gov.uk/output/Page3088.asp

38 Details at: http://www.un.org/apps/news/infocusnewsiraq.asp?NewsID=400&sID=8

39 'UNMOVIC-IAEA Press Statement on Inspection Activities in Iraq', 26 February
2003, at: http://www.un.org/apps/news/infocusnewsiraq.asp?NewsID=401&sID=8

40 For 27 February 2003, see
http://www.un.org/apps/news/infocusnewsiraq.asp?NewsID=403&sID=8. Links for
other dates on that page.

41 Oral introduction of the 12th quarterly report of UNMOVIC, 7 March 2003, at:
http://www.un.org/Depts/unmovic/SC7asdelivered.htm

42 James Bone, '6,000 gas bombs could be missing', *The Times*, 21 December 2002.

43 UNMOVIC, *Unresolved disarmament issues* (6 March 2003), p.50, at:
http://www.un.org/Depts/unmovic/new/documents/cluster_document.pdf;

44 'Briefing the Security Council, 19 December 2002: Inspections in Iraq and a preliminary
assessment of Iraq's weapons declaration', at:
http://www.un.org/Depts/unmovic/new/pages/security_council_briefings.asp

45 http://www.pm.gov.uk/output/Page3282.asp: 'Not a single interview has taken place
outside of Iraq, even though 1441 provided for it.'

46 Oral introduction of the 12th quarterly report of UNMOVIC, 7 March 2003, at:
http://www.un.org/Depts/unmovic/SC7asdelivered.htm

47 Thirteenth quarterly report of the Executive Chairman of the United Nations
Monitoring, Verification and Inspection Commission, 30 May 2003, at:
http://www.un.org/Docs/journal/asp/ws.asp?m=S/2003/580

48 http://www.number-10.gov.uk/output/Page3294.asp

49 UNMOVIC, *Unresolved disarmament issues* (6 March 2003), pp.104-05, at:
http://www.un.org/Depts/unmovic/new/documents/cluster_document.pdf

50 UNMOVIC, *Unresolved disarmament issues* (6 March 2003), p.82, at:
http://www.un.org/Depts/unmovic/new/documents/cluster_document.pdf

51 http://www.un.org/apps/news/infocusnewsiraq.asp?NewsID=414&sID=6

52 http://www.number-10.gov.uk/output/Page3448.asp; similarly, on 4 April 2003, at:
http://www.number-10.gov.uk/output/Page3434.asp

53 http://www.pm.gov.uk/output/Page3786.asp

54 http://www.pm.gov.uk/output/Page3803.asp

55 See, e.g., Douglas Jehl, 'Iraqi trailers said to make hydrogen, not biological arms', *New York Times*, 8 August 2003.

56 Hutton inquiry transcript, 14 August 2003, 16:7-8 and 17:8-10, at: http://www.the-hutton-inquiry.org.uk/content/transcripts/hearing-trans08.htm

57 Email from David Kelly to Judith Miller, 11 June 2003, at: http://www.the-hutton-inquiry.org.uk/content/com/com_4_0101to0104.pdf

58 http://www.pm.gov.uk/output/Page5025.asp

59 Quoted in Toby Helm, 'Bremer rejects Blair's 'secret labs' claim', *Daily Telegraph*, 29 December 2003.

60 Interim progress report on the activities of the Iraq Survey Group, 2 October 2003, at: http://www.cia.gov/cia/public_affairs/speeches/2003/david_kay_10022003.html

61 The transcript of the interview is available via: http://middleeastreference.org.uk/kamel.html

62 http://www.number-10.gov.uk/output/Page3088.asp. Similarly, in his speech of 15 February 2003, at a Labour Party conference in Glasgow, at: http://www.labour.org.uk/news/tbglasgow

63 http://www.number-10.gov.uk/output/Page3007.asp

64 Tony Blair, 'My Christian conscience is clear over war', *Independent on Sunday*, 2 March 2003.

65 UNSCOM report of 11 October 1995, para.11, at: http://www.un.org/Depts/unscom/sres95-864.htm

66 UNMOVIC, *Unresolved disarmament issues* (6 March 2003), p.160, at: http://www.un.org/Depts/unmovic/new/documents/cluster_document.pdf; UNSCOM report of 10 April 1995, paras.74 and 86, at: http://www.un.org/Depts/unscom/Semiannual/srep95-284.htm

67 United States Senate Select Committee on Intelligence, *Report on the U.S. Intelligence Community's Prewar Intelligence Assessments on Iraq* (7 July 2004), pp.65, 66.

68 As reported in, inter alia, David Leigh and Richard Norton-Taylor, 'Iraqi who gave MI6 45-minute claim says it was untrue', *The Guardian*, 27 January 2004; and Glenn Frankel and Rajiv Chandrasekaran, '45 minutes: behind the Blair claim', *Washington Post*, 29 February 2004.

69 BBC Breakfast with Frost, 21 April 2002. Transcript of interview at: http://news.bbc.co.uk/2/hi/programmes/breakfast_with_frost/1942222.stm

70 The major source of information on this individual is the United States Senate Select Committee on Intelligence, *Report on the U.S. Intelligence Community's Prewar Intelligence Assessments on Iraq* (7 July 2004), pp.152-57; also, Bob Drogin and Greg Miller, 'Iraqi Defector's Tales Bolstered U.S. Case for War', *Los Angeles Times*, 28 March 2004.

71 Butler report, §261.

72 Annex B of the Butler report, p.163, column 3.

73 Annex B of the Butler report, p.168, column 3.

74 Annex B of the Butler report, p.170, column 3.

75 Annex B of the Butler report, p.170, column 3.

76 Draft dossier of 19 September 2002, p.19; at http://www.the-hutton-inquiry.org.uk/content/cab/cab_3_0022to0078.pdf

77 Email of 19 September 2002. Reproduced at: http://www.the-hutton-inquiry.org.uk/content/cab/cab_11_0103.pdf

78 Text of 16 September 2002, reproduced at:
   http://www.the-hutton-inquiry.org.uk/content/cab/cab_11_0038to0040.pdf; and text of
   17 September 2002, reproduced at
   http://www.the-hutton-inquiry.org.uk/content/cab/cab_11_0047to0048.pdf

79 Note from Alastair Campbell to John Scarlett and others, 17 September 2002,
   reproduced at:
   http://www.the-hutton-inquiry.org.uk/content/cab/cab_11_0066to0068.pdf.
   Acknowledged by the Prime Minister in his evidence to the Hutton inquiry:
   transcript, 28 August 2003, 10:5-12, at:
   http://www.the-hutton-inquiry.org.uk/content/transcripts/hearing-trans22.htm.

80 Text of 17 September 2002, reproduced at:
   http://www.the-hutton-inquiry.org.uk/content/cab/cab_11_0064to0065.pdf

81 http://www.pm.gov.uk/output/Page3088.asp

82 http://www.pm.gov.uk/output/Page3294.asp

83 Press conference of 11 October 2002. Excerpt from transcript at:
   http://www.iraqwatch.org/government/UK/PMO/uk-pmo-blairputin-101102.htm

84 http://www.un.org/Depts/unmovic/new/pages/security_council_briefings.asp

85 http://www.un.org/apps/news/infocusnewsiraq.asp?NewsID=354&sID=6

86 http://www.pm.gov.uk/output/Page3005.asp

87 http://www.pm.gov.uk/output/Page1770.asp

88 http://www.pm.gov.uk/output/Page3294.asp

89 http://www.pm.gov.uk/output/Page5461.asp

90 Intelligence and Security Committee, *Iraqi Weapons of Mass Destruction –
   Intelligence and Assessments*, September 2003, §§126-27.

91 *Government Response to the Intelligence and Security Committee Report on Iraqi
   Weapons of Mass Destruction – Intelligence and Assessments*, 11 September 2003, §22.

92 The Butler report, §§285, 287.

93 http://www.publications.parliament.uk/pa/cm200203/cmselect/cmfaff/813/3062706.htm

94 http://www.iaea.org/NewsCenter/Statements/2003/ebsp2003n006.shtml

95 The same conclusion is repeated in the UNMOVIC statements of 9 December 2002
   and 17 January 2003:
   http://www.un.org/apps/news/infocusnewsiraq.asp?NewsID=284&sID=8 and
   http://www.un.org/apps/news/infocusnewsiraq.asp?NewsID=338&sID=8

96 'Inspectors Find Only Ruins at an Old Iraqi Weapons Site', *New York Times*, 29
   November 2002.

97 UNMOVIC, *Unresolved disarmament issues* (6 March 2003), p.116.

98 http://www.un.org/apps/news/infocusnewsiraq.asp?NewsID=382&sID=6

99 http://www.un.org/apps/news/infocusnewsiraq.asp?NewsID=414&sID=6

100 http://www.parliament.the-
    stationeryoffice.co.uk/pa/cm200203/cmhansrd/vo030319/text/30319w08.htm

101 http://www.pm.gov.uk/output/Page3803.asp

102 http://www.publications.parliament.uk/pa/cm200203/cmselect/cmliaisn/334-
    ii/3070802.htm

103 'Blair admits: I know my job is on the line', *The Observer*, 25 January 2004.

104 Hearing of the Senate Armed Services Committee, 28 January 2004. Transcript at:
    http://cns.miis.edu/cr/04_02_16.htm

105 http://www.publications.parliament.uk/pa/cm200304/cmselect/cmliaisn/310/4020303.htm

106 Daniel McGrory, 'New MI6 chief walks into storm over 'ties to Downing Street'',

The Times, 2 August 2004. The original allegation was made by Tom Mangold, 'Spy chief in new WMD cover-up', *Mail on Sunday*, 1 August 2004.

107 Julian Borger, 'Iraq survey group ignores Scarlett's WMD 'nuggets'', *The Guardian*, 5 August 2004.

108 Bryan Burrough et al., 'The path to war', *Vanity Fair*, May 2004, p.110.

109 Transcript at: http://usinfo.org/USIA/usinfo.state.gov/topical/pol/terror/02040502.htm

110 http://www.number-10.gov.uk/output/Page1711.asp

111 http://www.number-10.gov.uk/output/Page1712.asp

112 http://www.publications.parliament.uk/pa/cm200304/cmselect/cmdfence/57/3061104.htm

113 http://www.publications.parliament.uk/pa/cm200304/cmselect/cmdfence/57/3061103.htm

114 Quoted in the Butler report, §260.

115 Quoted in the Butler report, §268.

116 Quoted in the Butler report, §267.

117 Bryan Burrough et al., 'The path to war', *Vanity Fair*, May 2004, p.172.

118 Butler report, §286.

119 Butler report, §269.

120 Butler report, §288.

121 Bob Woodward, *Plan of Attack*, Simon & Schuster, 2004.

122 Bryan Burrough et al., 'The path to war', *Vanity Fair*, May 2004, p.172.

123 http://www.number-10.gov.uk/output/Page3088.asp

Chapter II References

124 1 HL Paper 43-1, HC 214-1, Session 1998-99

125 Standard Note: SN/PC/2666 Last updated: 18 September 2003 Parliament and Constitution Centre

126 1 HL Paper 43-1, HC 214-1, Session 1998-99

127 Holdsworth, William, A History of English Law 17th ed. Methuen 1957 Vol I, p379ff, Existing Criminal Jurisdiction of the House of Lords, Impeachment.

128 The Times, 4 March 1848; see also 5 and 25 February 1848

129 Hatsell, Precedents of Proceedings in the House of Commons, London 1796 Chapter The First p 71

130 Colin G Tite, Impeachment and Parliamentary Judicature in Early Stuart England, Athlone Press, University of London, 1974.

131 Holdsworth op cit p 383

132 Erskine May, Parliamentary Practice 19th ed pp 65-66

133 A.V. Dicey, E.C.S. Wade (Editor) Introduction to the Study of the Law of the Constitution p 441ff

134 Dicey op cit p443

135 FCO August 1999 and Halsbury's Laws of England, Vol 8(2) 4th ed. Miscellaneous powers of the Crown (1) The Making of treaties, Butterworth's 1996

136 C.E. Nicholson and Geoffrey Carnall eds, The Impeachment of Warren Hastings, Edinburgh University Press, 1989, Introduction.

137 Raoul Berger, Impeachment: The Constitutional Problems, Harvard 1974, preface

138 http://www.andrew-roberts.net/pages/books/eminent_churchillians.htm (August 2004)

139 Parliamentary Privilege Joint Committee First Report , 9 June 1997 http://www.publications.parliament.uk/cgi-bin/muscat_highlighter_first_match

140 Holdsworth op cit p.385

141 Colin Turpin, British Government and the Constitution, Butterworths, London.

142 Erskine May's Parliamentary Proceedings 1st ed p 374

143 HC Deb 2 November 1995 Vol 265 cc456-7

144 John Roskell The Impeachment of Michael de la Pole, Earl of Suffolk in 1386, Manchester University Press 1984

Annex B References

145 10 Downing Street Press Briefing: 3.45PM Thursday 1 April 2004

146 HC Deb 1 Apr 2004: Column 1754

147 http://news.bbc.co.uk/1/hi/uk_politics/1134709.stm, Wednesday, 24 January, 2001, 14:20 GMT, Mandelson's resignation statement

148 Prime Minister's Lobby Briefing: 3.35pm Wednesday 24 January 2001

149 HC Deb, 24 January 2001

150 Thursday December 24, 1998 The Guardian

Annex C References

151 Plucknett, 'Presidential Address' reproduced in 3 *Transactions, Royal Historical Society,* 5th Series, 145 (1952).

152 See *generally* C Roberts, *The Growth of Responsible Government in Stuart England* (Cambridge 1966).

153 Strafford was charged with treason, a term defined in 1352 by the Statute of Treasons, 25 Edw 3, stat. 5, c. 2 (1852). The particular charges against him presumably would have been within the compass of the general, or 'salvo,' clause of that statute, but did not fall within any of the enumerated acts of treason. Strafford rested his defence in part on that failure; his eloquence on the question of retrospective treasons ('Beware you do not awake these sleeping lions, by the searching out some neglected moth-eaten records, they may one day tear you and your posterity in pieces: it was your ancestors' care to chain them up within the barricades of statutes; be not you ambitious to be more skilful and curious that your forefathers in the art of killing.' *Celebrated Trials* 518 (Phila. 1837) may have dissuaded the Commons from bringing the trial to a vote in the House of Lords; instead they caused his execution by bill of attainder.

154 J. Rushworth, *The Tryal of Thomas Earl of Stafford*, in 8 Historical Collections 8 (1686).

155 Rushworth, *supra* n 4, at 8-9. R. Berger, *Impeachment: The Constitutional Problems* 30 (1973), states that the impeachment of Strafford' constitutes a great watershed in english constitutional history of which the Founders were aware.'

156 See *generally* A Simpson, *A Treatise on Federal Impeachments* 81-190 (Philadelphia, 1916), (Appendix of English Impeachment Trials); M.V. Clarke, 'The Origin of Impeachment' in Oxford Essays in Medieval History 164 (Oxford, 1934). Reading and analyzing the early history of English impeachments is complicated by the ambiguity of the records. The analysis that follows in this section has been drawn largely from the scholarship of others checked against the original records where possible. The basis for what became the impeachment procedure apparently originated in 1341, when the King and Parliament alike accepted the principle that the King's ministers were to answer in Parliament for their misdeeds. C. Roberts, *supra* n. 2, at 7. Offences against Magna Carta, for example, were failing for technicalities

in the ordinary courts, and therefore Parliament provided that offenders against Magan Carta be declared in Parliament and judged by their peers. Clarke, *supra*, at 173.

157 Simpson, *supra* n. 6. at 86; Berger, *supra* n.5, at 61; Adams and Stevens, *Select Documents of English Constitutional History* 148 (London 1927).

158 For example, de la Pole was charged with purchasing property of great value from the King while using his position as Chancellor to have the lands appraised at less that they were worth, all in violation of his oath, in deceit of the King and in neglect of the need of the realm. Adams and Stevens, *supra* n. 7. at 148.

159 Adams and Stevens, *supra* n.7, at 148-150.

160 4 *Hatsell* 67 (Shannon, Ireland, 1971, reprint of London 1796, 1818).

161 4 *Hatsell*, *supra* n.10 at 67, charges 2, 6 and 12.

162 The Long Parliament (1640-48) alone impeached 98 persons. Roberts, *supra* n. 2, at 133.

163 2 *Howell State Trials* 1135,1136-37 (charges 1,2, and 6). See *generally* Simpson, *supra* n. 6, at 91-127; Berger, *supra* n. 5, at 67-73.

164 Peter Pett, Commissioner of the Navy, was charged in 1668 with negligent preparation for an invasion by the Dutch, and negligent loss of a ship. The latter charge was predicated on alleged wilful neglect in failing to insure that the ship was brought to mooring 6 *Howell State Trials* 865, 866-67 (charges 1, 5).

165 Chief Justice Scroggs was charged in 1680, among other things, with browbeating witnesses and commenting on their credibility, and with cursing and drinking to excess, thereby bringing 'the highest scandal on the public justice of the kingdom.' 8 *Howell State Trials* 197, 200 (charges 7,8).

166 Simpson, *supra* n.6, at 144.

167 Simpson, *supra* n.6, at 144.

168 See *generally* Marshall, *The Impeachment of Warren Hastings* (Oxford, 1965).

169 Of the original resolutions proposed by Edmund Burke in 1786 and accepted by the House as articles of impeachment in 1787, both criminal and non-criminal offences appear. The fourth article, for example, charging that Hastings had confiscated the landed income of the Begums of Oudh, was described by Pitt as that of all others that bore the strongest marks of criminality. Marshall, *supra* n. 19, at 53.

The third article, on the other hand, known as the Benares charge, claimed that circumstances imposed upon the Governor-General a duty to conduct himself 'on the most distinguished principles of good faith, equity, moderation, and mildness.' Instead, continued the charge, Hastings provoked a revolt in Benares, resulting in 'the arrest of the rajah, three revolutions in the country and great loss, whereby the said Hastings is guilty of a high crime and misdemeanour in the destruction of the country aforesaid.' The common, *supra* n. 6, at 168-170; Marshall, supra n. 19, at xv, 46.

170 See *e.g.,* Berger, *supra* n.5, at 70-71.

171 Berger, *supra* n.5, at 62.

Opinion

In the matter of an impeachment of the Prime Minister arising from the war against Iraq

Rabinder Singh QC
Prof. Conor Gearty

Introduction and Summary

1. We are asked to advise on the legal issues arising out of the possible impeachment of the Prime Minister Mr Tony Blair MP ('the Prime Minister') for misleading Parliament and the public on the issue of the intelligence that supported the case for war in Iraq.

2. In summary, for the reasons set out below, our opinion is that:

(1) The power of impeachment is one which is still available to Parliament as a matter of law.

(2) Its use is appropriate where there is a prima facie case (i.e. a case to answer) of either crimes or serious breaches of constitutional principles.

(3) There is, on the material before us, a case to answer that the Prime Minister was guilty of a serious breach of constitutional principles.

(4) There are prescribed procedures for instituting an impeachment, which are outlined further below.

3. In constructing his request for this Opinion, our instructing solicitor ('IS') has requested that a number of specific questions be answered, and we have organised our Opinion accordingly. Before we turn to those specific questions we set out below our understanding of the law and practice relating to impeachment generally.

4. This Opinion should be read with *A Case to Answer: A First Report on the Potential Impeachment of the Prime Minister for High Crimes and Misdemeanours in relation to the Invasion of Iraq* ('A Case to Answer' – see pages 11-83 above)[1]. In what follows we refer to this document where necessary rather than reproducing here the evidence that is already covered there more fully.

The law and practice on impeachment

5. The leading scholarly texts on impeachment are unclear as to the exact basis required for the laying of such a charge. *Halsbury's Laws of England* refers to impeachment as being available 'for any crime whatever',[2] but in the immediately following paragraph refers to the motion of impeachment as involving allegations of 'high crimes and misdemeanours',[3] neither of which terms is defined. In its 1st edition, where the subject is treated extensively, *Erskine May* refers to 'great public offences',[4] to 'high treason .. certain high crimes and misdemeanours'[5] and to the need for the Commons to 'find the crime'.[6] It is also said that the procedure 'is reserved for extraordinary crimes and extraordinary offenders.'[7]

6. In his classic work, *A History of English Law*,[8] Sir William Holdsworth referred to the 'efficacy' of the process as being dependent upon its being 'strictly limited to prosecuting offenders against the law'.[9] He defined impeachment as 'a criminal proceeding initiated by the House of Commons against any person'.[10] The last four impeachments, according to Holdsworth, 'were not occasioned by the political conduct of the accused, who were all charged with serious breaches of the criminal law'.[11] But Holdsworth clearly saw the jurisdiction as not limited to the ordinary criminal law; he contemplated its use for wrongdoings of a much broader nature, including 'corruption, gross negligence or other misfeasances in the conduct of the affairs of the nation'.[12] The process was a criminal one but this did not mean that the conduct against which it was rightly focused needed to be criminal under some other law.

7. On the other hand the scholarly authorities suggest that the procedure should not be taken too far. Holdsworth considered that: '[s]o soon as the aim of the Commons came to be, not only to secure the observance of the law by the king's ministers, but also to secure their adhesion to the line of policy which they approved, the weakness of impeachment as a constitutional weapon began to appear.'[13] This would seem to indicate that, while the charge of impeachment is theoretically very broad, it should be confined to wrongs of a legal, or at least of a serious constitutional, nature.

8. The extension of impeachment to constitutional as well as criminal matters is supported by precedent. In his well-known work, *The Constitutional History of Modern Britain since 1485*,[14] Sir D L Keir does not essay a definition of impeachment but does point out that the charge against Earl Strafford had been that he was minded to 'subvert the fundamental laws and governance of the realms of England and Ireland ... by giving His Majesty advice by force of arms ...'.[15] Other examples of the breadth of the process can be identified by examination of the precedents.[16]

9. The proposition that impeachment extends beyond the criminal into the constitutional sphere is also supported by consideration of the rationale of the process, and by an examination of why its use has lapsed in recent years.

10. As far as the first of these is concerned, in his *Constitutional History of*

England,[17] F W Maitland, arguably England's greatest ever legal historian, was clearly of the view that impeachment had a remit wider than the assertion of an alternative criminal jurisdiction focusing only on breaches of the ordinary criminal law. To Maitland, 'it was as a check upon the King's Ministers that the impeachment was chiefly valuable, and came to be afterwards valued ...'[18] After the process had fallen into disuse for nearly 200 years, it was 'evident' that in its revival in 1621 'parliament ha[d] unearthed a weapon of enormous importance'.[19]

11. Holdsworth thought impeachment 'a law which could do justice even when the ordinary law failed.'[20] Examining its origins, Holdsworth considered that the 'practice of impeachment arose partly from the prevalent political ideal – government according to law.'[21] On this view, the process of impeachment exists to provide a measure of accountability to Parliament.

12. *Erskine May* takes the same line: impeachment is 'the great representative inquest of the nation'[22] and 'an instrument of popular power and for the furtherance of public justice'.[23] The process extends to 'high crimes and misdemeanours, beyond the reach of the law, or which no other authority in the state will prosecute'.[24] It is 'a safeguard of public liberty well worthy of a free country, and of so noble an institution as a free Parliament'.[25] Though the language is restricted to criminal law in these passages, as we have already indicated above, the remit of the process is not explicitly restricted to the criminal sphere: the commission of a criminal act without any accountability is a particular (and egregious) example of the kind of official impunity which it was the historic purpose of the impeachment jurisdiction to seek to curtail and control.

13. Turning now to the second point identified at para. 9 above, related to the decline of impeachment, Holdsworth's explanation was that 'it ceased to be necessary to use it for political purposes when it became possible to get rid of ministers by an adverse vote of the House of Commons'.[26] Maitland was against the use of impeachment in the modern era because '[i]f a statesman has really committed a crime then he can be tried like any other criminal: if he has been guilty of some misdoing that is not a crime ... [then] for such misdoings disgrace and loss of office are now-a-days sufficient punishments.'[27] Clearly this position was based on the assumption that such punishments are meted out.

14. In the context of this discussion both of the historic rationale and the decline of impeachment, a further, highly authoritative writer may now be referred to. In his *Introduction to the Study of the Law of the Constitution,*[28] Professor A V Dicey located his discussion of impeachment squarely within his chapter on the responsibility of ministers. Professor Dicey regarded impeachment as '[i]n some instances ... the only legal mode in which [a Minister's] offence could be reached'.[29] By offence here Dicey was referring to illegal acts where for some reason or another liability to 'criminal or civil proceedings in a court of law' was not possible.[30] But he also saw impeachment as available historically for 'violations of the constitution'.[31] For Dicey as for

Holdsworth and Maitland, it was because of the rise of alternative forms of accountability that 'this mode of enforcing Ministerial responsibility [was] almost out of date'.[32] This is how Dicey put it:

How is it that the ancient methods of enforcing Parliamentary authority, such as impeachment, the formal refusal of supplies, and the like, have fallen into disuse?

The answer is, that they are disused because ultimate obedience to the underlying principle of all modern constitutionalism, which is nothing else than the principle of obedience to the will of the nation as expressed through Parliament, is so closely bound up with the law of the land that it can hardly be violated without a breach of the ordinary law. Hence the extraordinary remedies, which were once necessary for enforcing the deliberate will of the nation, having become unnecessary, have fallen into desuetude. If they are not altogether abolished, the cause lies partly in the conservatism of the English people, and partly in the valid consideration that crimes may still be committed for which the ordinary law of the land hardly affords due punishment, and which therefore may well be dealt with by the High Court of Parliament.[33]

15. Writing in the same spirit, Holdsworth thought that impeachment 'might still be a useful weapon in the armoury of the constitution' since it 'does embody the sound principle that ministers and officials should be made criminally liable for corruption, gross negligence or other misfeasances in the conduct of the affairs of the nation'.[34] In a passage of immediate and direct relevance, Holdsworth continued:

And this principle requires to be emphasised at a time when the development of the system of party government pledges the party to defend the policy of its leaders, however mistaken it may be, and however incompetently it may have been carried out; at a time when party leaders are apt to look indulgently on the most disastrous mistakes, because they hope that the same indulgence will be extended to their own mistakes when they take office; at a time when the principle of the security of the tenure of higher permanent officials is held to be more important than the need to publish their negligences and ignorances. If ministers were sometimes made criminally responsible for gross negligence or rashness, ill considered activities might be discouraged, real statesmanship might be encouraged, and party violence might be moderated.[35]

16. It would seem to follow that in the view of these writers, the continuing disuse of impeachment is not an inevitable state of affairs but is, rather, contingent on the continuation of those other, alternative forms of public accountability which have come over time to take its place.

17. From the foregoing summary of the foremost constitutional authorities on impeachment, it is possible to derive the following propositions:

(i) As a matter of strict law, the procedure of impeachment is potentially available to be used by Parliament for any perceived wrong whatsoever, and against anyone, but as a matter of constitutional propriety the process should only be deployed in a narrower range of situations.

(ii) The situations in which it is constitutionally appropriate to initiate the process of impeachment are deducible by reference to the underlying rationale of the procedure, which is to hold government to account.

(iii) Impeachment is appropriate where there is no other means of calling a person to account, either legally or politically, for some serious wrong that he or she has done. In practice only Ministers of the Crown are potentially free of legal and/or political accountability in this way, so they are the only category of persons against whom it is appropriate to initiate this kind of proceedings.

(iv) The kind of serious wrong envisaged at (iii) above undoubtedly encompasses the commission of *serious criminal offences*. The authorities discussed above suggest that it also extends to other *serious breaches of the constitution*.

(v) For initiation of the procedure of impeachment to be appropriate, there must first be prima facie evidence of such wrongdoing (*'the evidential threshold'*).[36] But there must also be, secondly, evidence of the lack of any alternative legal or political accountability for such action (*'the impunity threshold'*), the operation of which – if it exists – being much preferable to the process of impeachment which is a residual blunderbuss, to be held in reserve until all else has failed, and been seen to fail.

Question 1: Evidence: is there a case to answer?

18. Given the state of the law on impeachment set out above, there is a case for the Prime Minister to answer, based on the following serious breach of constitutional propriety for which there is no other form of accountability –legal or political[37] – known to the British constitution:

Misleading Parliament as to the basis for military action against Iraq so as to obtain from that body (and its individual members) support for the conflict which would not necessarily have been forthcoming, in contravention of the fundamental constitutional principle of ministerial accountability to Parliament.

19. The evidence in support of this view is set out in the Report *A Case to Answer*, especially Chapter 1, section 1 ('the Prime Minister's statements on Iraq that were unsupported by the intelligence assessments available to him'); section 2 ('failure to disclose available counter-evidence, and to ensure claims were verified') and section 3 ('failure to withdraw material found to be false, or which should have been found to be false'). We summarise the contents of Chapter 1 of the Report by reference to the executive summary in para. 2 of the Introduction:

The first chapter of the report examines the statements and actions of the Prime Minister from September 2001 to August 2004 relating to Iraq. In particular, it finds that the Prime Minister:

- exaggerated the condition of Iraq's illicit weapons well beyond the assessments of the intelligence services or the United Nations inspectors. He asserted in early 2002 that Iraq had 'stockpiles of major amounts of chemical and biological weapons', whilst the assessment of the Joint Intelligence Committee at the time was that Iraq 'may have hidden small quantities of agents and weapons' (section 1.1);

- claimed that 'Saddam Hussein poses a severe threat not just to the region, but to the wider world' and had 'enough chemical and biological weapons remaining to devastate the entire Gulf region', whilst the intelligence assessment was that 'Saddam has not succeeded in seriously threatening his neighbours' (section 1.2);

- asserted that the 'UN proved' he had chemical and biological weapons because they were unaccounted for, in contrast to the warning by the executive chairman of UNMOVIC Hans Blix that 'One must not jump to the conclusion that they [weapons that were unaccounted for] exist' (section 1.3);

- claimed that Iraq's 'WMD programme is active, detailed and growing', even though he later admitted to the Butler review team that intelligence showed that 'what had changed was not the pace of Iraq's prohibited weapons programmes, which had not been dramatically stepped up' (section 1.4).

- insisted that the invasion of Iraq was lawful because Iraq had committed a 'material breach' of Security Council Resolution 1441 by not cooperating with inspectors, even though Hans Blix told the Security Council that 'the numerous initiatives, which are now taken by the Iraqi side with a view to resolving some long-standing open disarmament issues, can be seen as "active", or even "proactive"' (section 1.5).

- claimed after the invasion that 'our intelligence' had confirmed that Iraq's 'two mobile biological weapons facilities' were part of a larger set of such facilities, even though intelligence had yet to examine the trailers, and then found them unconnected to biological weapons programmes (section 1.6);

- held back crucial information from intelligence sources that indicated that Iraq had destroyed its weapons stockpile (section 2.1);

- failed to ensure that intelligence sources were adequately checked, even when straightforward measures could have been taken to check those sources (section 2.2);

- claimed that the intelligence available to him was 'extensive, detailed and authoritative', even though he had been briefed by the Chief of MI6 about how key sources should be treated with caution (section 2.3);

- did not reveal the intelligence assessment in his possession that Iraq would be unlikely to use chemical or biological weapons outside its territory unless attacked first, despite the significance of this assessment (section 2.4);

- declared that the Iraqi declaration of December 2002 was 'false', even though he had not asked for that declaration to be analysed fully by the intelligence services (section 2.5);

- warned that 'it is a matter of time unless we act and take a stand before terrorism and weapons of mass destruction come together', even though the intelligence assessment was that the 'greatest terrorist threat to Western interests ... would be heightened by military action against Iraq', and the government was later forced to admit that 'the JIC assessed that any collapse of the Iraqi regime would increase the risk of chemical and biological warfare technology or agents finding their way in to the hands of terrorists, and that the Prime Minister was aware of this' (section 2.6);

- claimed in March 2003 that the contents of the September dossier 'still accurately reflect our assessment of the position with regard to Iraq's proscribed weapons programmes', even though those inspectors found a large number of the claims in it to be false (section 3.1);

- affirmed in January 2004 that 'the intelligence we received [prior to the war] is correct', even though the intelligence services had raised doubts about at least four key sources from at least six months earlier (section 3.2); and

- gave his support to the then chair of the Joint Intelligence Committee in interfering with the compilation of a report by the Iraq Survey Group, with the aim of preventing the extent of past mistakes from being made public (section 3.3).

20. We agree with what is said at para 5 of the Introduction to the Report: 'It is for Parliament to decide whether the Prime Minister should be impeached. We consider that this report shows that there is a case of impeachable offences for the Prime Minister to answer.'

Question 2: Does the remedy of impeachment still exist or is it formally obsolete?

21. Our view is that the procedure of impeachment still exists. It may have 'fallen into disuse' as the most recent edition of *Erskine May* suggests,[38] but the foregoing analysis points clearly to its continuing existence and potential utility. As *Halsbury's Laws* notes, the jurisdiction has not been abolished.[39]

22. The Select Committee on Parliamentary Privilege which reported in 1967 was clear that legislation would be needed to formally abandon the jurisdiction.[40] No such legislation has been enacted.[41]

Question 3: Can the Speaker refuse to accept a motion and supporting proofs? What are the Speaker's Options?

23. Any member may move a motion, possibly but not necessarily supported by a speech.[42] The rules governing notice of motions are set out in the latest edition of *Erskine May*.[43]

24. *Erskine May* notes that the Speaker may refuse 'to propose the question upon motions and amendments which are irregular'.[44] A direct and clear notice of motion of impeachment of the Prime Minister would be necessary in order for the motion not to be ruled to be irregular.[45] Early day motions (if this is the route that is chosen) should not generally exceed 250 words.[46] The motion should not

contain unbecoming expressions, infringe the House's rules, or be otherwise irregular.[47]

Question 4: If the Speaker can and does refuse to accept a motion and proofs what, if any, remedy is available to MPs?

25. A motion goes first to the Clerk at the Table. If it is refused, the Member is informed and has the right to refer the matter to the Speaker. If the Speaker upholds the Clerk's opinion, the Member is entitled to see the Speaker to argue his or her case further. If the Member is still dissatisfied, then he or she can raise the matter in the House by way of a motion.[48]

26. According to the leading scholarly work on the proceedings of Parliament, '[a]ny member may give notice, and have it printed on the Order Paper ... [on] almost any motion on any subject', with all that is being required is that the motion be expressed in proper parliamentary language and be a 'proper subject for debate'.[49]

Question 5: If he must accept the motion and proofs and he does so what must the Commons do before deciding whether the mover of the motion should go to the bar of the House of Lords?

27. After a motion has been agreed to by the House of Commons, the mover is 'instructed to go to the House of Lords and impeach the offender of high crimes and misdemeanours and acquaint the Lords that the Commons "will, in due time, exhibit particular articles against him, and make good the same"'.[50] Such a motion may be put more quickly than its proposer desires: under Standing Order No 29 (power of Chair to propose question), 'when a Member is in the course of making a motion or moving an amendment at any stage of proceedings on a bill, a Member rising in his place may claim to move "That the question be now proposed" and, unless it appears to the Chair that the motion is an abuse of the rules of the House, that question shall be put forthwith by the Chair. It is not debatable.'[51]

Questions 6-9: If the matter goes to the Lords (i) what are the relevant rules?; (ii) who draws up the articles?; and (iii) what is the role of the movers, Parliamentary Counsel, the Commons, the Lords and Counsel to the PM etc?

28. The House of Commons appoints a committee to draw up the articles of impeachment for the approval of the House. These are usually drawn up after the motion has been passed but can be done before this, as they were in the case of Warren Hastings. The Commons then send the articles to the Lords while reserving the right to send further articles if the Commons think them necessary; and the Lords make an order for a copy of the articles to be granted to the accused person, to each of which he is directed to put in his answer within a specified time.[52]

29. As soon as the articles of impeachment have been exhibited the accused

may be attached. In the case of the Prime Minister, as a member of the House of Commons, the task of arresting him would devolve on the Serjeant-at-Arms and he would keep the Prime Minister in custody until such time as the Lords ordered the Gentleman Usher of the Black Rod to take the accused into custody. Bail is however a possibility.[53]

30. The day for the hearing is fixed by the House of Lords. As the Prime Minister is a commoner, the Lord Chancellor would preside. The Commons attend the trial as a committee of the whole House, and their case is put forward by certain of their members whom the House would appoint as its managers to prepare the evidence and conduct the prosecution on its behalf. The accused person may summon witnesses and may be heard by counsel.[54]

31. All members of the House of Lords are equally judges of law and fact. The Lord Chancellor would be present only to regulate procedure and is a judge to no greater an extent than any other lord. In determining whether the charges have been proved, each article of the impeachment is taken separately, the Lord Chancellor asking each peer in turn (by precedent beginning with the junior baron) whether the defendant is guilty or not guilty, and then announcing the result.[55]

32 If the accused is declared to be guilty, he may plead further matters in arrest of judgment; and in no case is judgment delivered by the Lords until it has been demanded by the Speaker on behalf of the Commons.[56]

33. A royal pardon is possible after but not before conviction.[57]

34. Impeachment proceedings are not brought to an end by the dissolution of Parliament.[58]

Question 10: Can MPs put pressure during an impeachment process for the testing of the evidence from an alternative route, namely a judicial inquiry if not through a full impeachment trial?

35. The motion of impeachment could ask for an order remitting the matter to a panel of judges for decision. This was suggested during an earlier trial for impeachment, of Sir Adam Blair in 1689, but was rejected by the Lords.[59]

Question 11: If MPs are excluded from proper debate do they have grounds to make a complaint to the European Court of Human Rights?

36. This is highly unlikely. Even if a clear transgression of the right to freedom of expression were established, in itself highly unlikely given the many other avenues for such debate and the fact that the controls were being placed by the legislative body on its own members, the European Court of Human Rights is very unlikely to regard dispute as to what is proper for discussion in Parliament as within its remit.[60] So far as domestic law is concerned, the duty imposed on public authorities by section 6(1) of the Human Rights Act 1998, to act in a way which is compatible with Convention rights, is not applicable to 'either House of Parliament or a person exercising functions in connection with proceedings in Parliament': section 6(3).

37. The issue of ensuring that the trial of impeachment is not conducted in a way which infringes the Prime Minister's rights under the European Convention on Human Rights is a matter which has not been addressed in this Opinion. However, we draw attention again to section 6(3) of the Human Rights Act, which we have cited above.

Conclusion

38. If we can be of further assistance our Instructing Solicitor should not hesitate to contact us again.

Rabinder Singh QC
Professor Conor Gearty
17 September 2004

Opinion References

1 Produced for Adam Price MP by Glen Rangwala and Dan Plesch, August 2004.

2 *Laws of England* 4th edn, vol 10 reissue (2002), para [355].

3 Ibid para [356].

4 Sir T Erskine May, *A Treatise on the Law, Privileges, Proceedings and Usage of Parliament*, 1st edn (1844) p 39.

5 Ibid 376.

6 Ibid 38.

7 Ibid 375.

8 7th edn eds A L Goodhart, H G Hanbury, and S B Chrimes, (London, 1956)

9 Ibid vol 1, p 383.

10 Ibid p 379. See also vol 6 p 260, where it is asserted 'that a man ought no more to be found guilty upon an impeachment than he ought upon an indictment, unless some definite crime could be proved against him'.

11 Ibid vol 1, p 384. Holdsworth had in mind the impeachments of Lord Macclesfield (1724), Lord Lovat (1746), Warren Hastings (1787) and Lord Melville (1805).

12 Ibid, 385.

13 Ibid p 383

14 9th edn, London, 1969.

15 Ibid p 213.

16 See generally *Precedents of proceedings in the House of Commons, Mr Hatsell's precedents* (London, 1796); *A Case to Answer*, ch 2.5.5.

17 Cambridge, 1926.

18 Ibid p 215.

19 Ibid 246.

20 n 8 above vol 1 p 380.

21 Ibid p 381.

22 n 4 above p 38.

23 Ibid p 39.

24 Ibid 374.

25 Ibid.

26 n 8 above, p 384.

27 n 17 above p 477.

28 10th edn by E C S Wade (London, 1959).

29 Ibid p 327.

30 Ibid 326-327.

31 See esp ibid p 443

32 Ibid 327.

33 Ibid 454-455.

34 n 8 above vol 1 p 385

35 ibid

36 An analogy can be drawn with criminal procedure, so that there will be a case to answer if a reasonable tribunal could, on the evidence, find the charge proved. This is what we mean by a prima facie case.

37 On which see for further details of the degree of impunity *A Case to Answer* n 1 above, ch 2.4

38 23rd edn (London, 2004), p 73.

39 n 2 above, para [355].

40 See para [115] of the Report, and further Parl Debates, House of Commons, 4 July 1969, cols 827-828 (Mr F Peart).

41 For the disciplinary powers of Parliament see First Report of the Parliamentary Joint Committee on Parliamentary Privilege, HL 43, HC 214, Session 1998-99, ch 6.

42 n 38 above, p 381.

43 Ibid, pp 382-393.

44 Ibid p 221.

45 See ibid pp 386-387: motions relating to members of either House must be by way of substantive motion.

46 Ibid p 390.

47 Ibid.

48 The procedure is set out at ibid.

49 Griffth and Ryle, *Parliament* (2nd edn by Blackburn and Kennon), ch 6-074.

50 *Halsbury*, n 2 above, para [356].

51 *Erskine May*, n 38 above, p 392.

52 *Halsbury*, n 2 above, para [356].

53 Ibid n1, referring to the case of the Earl of Oxford (20 *Lords Journal* 112) and the case of Dr Sacheverell (16 *Commons Journal* 242).

54 Ibid para [356]

55 Ibid.

56 Ibid.

57 *Erskine May*, n 4 above, p 380.

58 Ibid p 379

59 Ibid p 376

60 See *Demicoli v Malta* (1992) 14 EHRR 47, para. 33, where a contrast is drawn between members of a legislative body and members of the public.

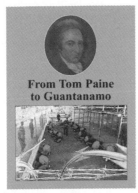
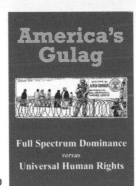

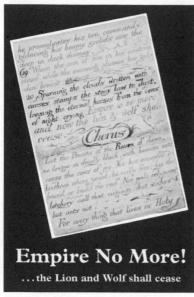